ARMY LIFE ON THE WESTERN FRONTIER

ARMY LIFE ON THE

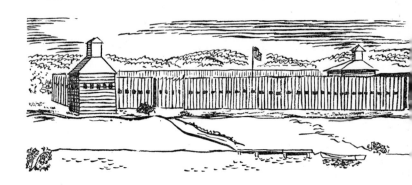

Edited by Francis Paul Prucha

WESTERN FRONTIER

*Selections from the Official Reports
Made Between 1826 and 1845 by
Colonel George Croghan*

NORMAN
UNIVERSITY OF OKLAHOMA PRESS

By Francis Paul Prucha

Broadax and Bayonet: The Role of the United States Army in the Development of the Northwest, 1815–1860. Madison, Wis., 1953.

(Editor) *Army Life on the Western Frontier: Selections from the Official Reports Made Between 1826 and 1845 by Colonel George Croghan.* Norman, 1958.

85079

355.12

C941a

Library of Congress Catalog Card Number 58–11600
Copyright 1958 by the University of Oklahoma Press,
Publishing Division of the University.
Composed and printed at Norman, Oklahoma, U.S.A.,
by the University of Oklahoma Press.
First edition.

TO MY FATHER

PREFACE

THIS BOOK is intended to augment our knowledge of the United States Army on the frontier. The selections it contains are the official inspection reports of a pre–Civil War inspector general, who for many years was a discerning visitor at the western forts. George Croghan was an old soldier, whose military-mindedness sharpened all his remarks; in his reports we have a valuable record of the early western garrisons and their contribution to America's westward advance.

In an age of two world wars the wartime exploits of the American army have been subjected to careful historical research, and accounts of these events have appeared in well written and attractively published books. But the army in peacetime has not as yet received adequate treatment. This is especially to be regretted in regard to the frontier, where the army played a more than preparatory role. The peacetime army of today is considered only in terms of its war potential; in earlier decades of our history, the peacetime army in its own right made important contributions to American development. For decades the army defended the outer edge of the advancing frontier. It stimulated settlement and civilization and was an important force in the development of our nation, yet it has all but passed into oblivion.

In the selections printed here the exact wording of the

original has been retained, and older spellings, if correct, have not been changed. Contractions, however, have been expanded, excessive capitalization dropped, and punctuation modified when necessary for clarity or smoother reading. Spellings of certain common words have been made uniform in order to avoid confusion. Particularly long paragraphs have been broken at convenient spots. The resulting text still shows inconsistencies, for the scribes of a century ago did not follow a strictly uniform practice any more than their descendants do. Croghan himself was not always consistent in spelling or grammatical usage, and the multiplication of the clerks who transcribed his reports multiplied the variations.

The reports included here have been selected with a view toward presenting typical comments, eliminating at the same time monotonous repetition of similar items. Special remarks on such topics as military discipline or Indian affairs, which Croghan appended to his routine reports, have in most cases been included.

My sincere thanks to the persons who helped make this book possible—to archivists and librarians who dug out data and illustrations, to the colleague who searched through documents I myself was unable to examine, and to friends who shared the tasks of collating the typescript with the original manuscripts and reading proofs.

Francis Paul Prucha

St. Marys, Kansas
March 3, 1958

CONTENTS

ILLUSTRATIONS

Map

INTRODUCTION

F OR SEVERAL decades after the War of 1812 the western
rivers marked the general limits of the frontier. On this
frontier, along the Mississippi and its tributaries, the army
established a series of military outposts as visible signs of
American authority. These garrisons were to overawe the
Indians and prevent outbreaks of hostility and to afford
refuge and security in the event of Indian wars. Small, isolated, and insignificant in terms of fortification, the posts
nevertheless made an outstanding contribution to western
development, as a stabilizing and moderating force in the
dramatic effort of settling the continent. During the period
of American history to which Frederick Jackson Turner gave
the name "the rise of the new West" these army forts stood
firm. They were tiny citadels in the vast wilderness, but they
were also mighty weapons in the spread of United States
authority and culture toward the west.

It is difficult for the modern mind to picture the life and
activities of these posts. The total strength of the army was
set by Congress in 1821 at six thousand men, but the authorized strength was never quite reached in actuality because
of the delay in recruiting and the heavy desertion. And the
troops had to be dispersed along a 2,000-mile seaboard and
an equally long Indian frontier in the West. The result was

a series of small posts strung like beads along the Atlantic and scattered up and down the western rivers according to the actual or estimated needs of the day.[1]

Each post was cut off from the world, except for the periodic supply boats or the mail couriers who arrived by steamboat, by canoe, or overland on foot. Each post, however, was visited regularly—annually if possible—by an inspector general, who checked the behavior of the garrison against the pertinent army regulations and forwarded reports of his findings to the General-in-chief in Washington. By this means, in age-old army fashion, was some semblance of military spirit and discipline maintained at wilderness outposts, where the military spirit was being constantly corroded by the isolation, the heavy work of garrison building, road construction, farming, and fuel gathering, and the resulting neglect in soldierly instruction.

For twenty years of this critical period of American expansion the man who inspected the western forts was Colonel George Croghan. His firsthand reports on the forts—frank, incisive, sometimes laudatory, often critical, but always sparked by a military spirit—provide one of the best and most intimate pictures of these vanguard garrisons.

Croghan, who was born near Louisville, Kentucky, on November 15, 1791, was marked by devotion to the military life.

---

[1] A factual account of the posts on the frontier in the period before the Mexican War can be found in Henry P. Beers, *The Western Military Frontier, 1815–1846* (Philadelphia, 1935). For army activities in the West in the decade following the War of 1812 see Edgar B. Wesley, *Guarding the Frontier: A Study of Frontier Defense from 1815 to 1825* (Minneapolis, 1935). Francis Paul Prucha, *Broadax and Bayonet: The Role of the United States Army in the Development of the Northwest, 1815–1860* (Madison, 1953), and Grant Foreman, *Advancing the Frontier*, 1830–1860 (Norman, 1933), supply information about the posts in the upper Mississippi Valley and the old Southwest respectively.

His mother was the sister of George Rogers Clark and William Clark, and their courage and spirit were early exhibited in the young man. His father, William Croghan, had been an officer in the Revolution and retained the title of "Major." Memoirs of George's early childhood tell us that even then he loved military things. Although he graduated from the College of William and Mary in 1810 and had his eye on the law, he was soon winning praise as a volunteer in campaigns against the Indians.[2]

The high esteem in which Croghan was held appears in a letter written by General William Henry Harrison to the Secretary of War early in 1812. The General recommended the young man for a captaincy in the army, as a soldier "who certainly conducted himself in the most exemplary manner, in every station in which he served." Harrison continued: "Although brought up with all the delicacy that is common in [an] affluent family, he performed all the duties of a private Dragoon, with the most zealous assiduity; and was always amongst the foremost to volunteer his services in the fatigue parties, that were called on to work on the New Post, on which he laboured many days although his Corps was exempted from the fatigue detail. I can also assert that he possesses all the courage and fire which are so necessary to form a good officer."[3] Even if we discount the ebullience that generally marks such a letter of recommendation, this is still high praise. The confidence was not misplaced, as George

[2] The sources for biographical data on Croghan are indicated in the bibliographical notes, pages 173–74. The George Croghan who is the subject of this book should not be confused with the eighteenth-century Indian trader of the same name.

[3] William Henry Harrison to Secretary of War William Eustis, January 6, 1812, in Croghan Papers, volume 1, in the Draper Collection of the State Historical Society of Wisconsin.

Croghan proved by his heroic role in the War of 1812. The "courage and fire which are so necessary to form a good officer" were certainly there in abundance, and although Croghan's peacetime work as inspector general was forgotten, the fame of his wartime heroism has only slowly died away.

Croghan, a major in the Seventeenth Infantry, was in command of Fort Stephenson at Lower Sandusky (now the city of Fremont, Ohio) as the British general, Henry Proctor, advanced. The fort, according to the general consensus, could not be held against the British, and there were standing orders to evacuate the fort if the British advanced with artillery. Croghan was determined, however, not to retreat, and he held his post even after General Harrison had sent new orders to destroy the post and withdraw. Croghan made so strong a case for his action that he won over General Harrison. The small garrison repulsed Proctor, and George Croghan was a national hero. The American people, hungry for some victory in a war which was not going well, caught up the defense of Fort Stephenson as a major event, and with it the young Major was rocketed to fame. Papers throughout the country were full of his name; he was brevetted lieutenant colonel for his bravery, and a new sword was presented to him by the ladies of Chillicothe.[4]

[4] For accounts of the defense of Fort Stephenson see Robert B. McAfee, *History of the Late War in the Western Country* (reprint of original 1816 edition, Bowling Green, 1919), 344–55, and Benson J. Lossing, *The Pictorial Field-book of the War of 1812* (New York, 1869), 499–504. Croghan himself criticized McAfee's account of the defense of Fort Stephenson and carried on an animated correspondence about the matter with General Harrison, who approved the book. See the correspondence between the two men, July 1, 1818, to December 20, 1825, in Croghan Family Papers, Library of Congress.

The Croghan Papers in the Draper Collection contain many letters of George Croghan to his father, written during the War of 1812. See also the references listed in footnote 6 below, since the writings dealing with Croghan the hero contain descriptions of the defense of Fort Stephenson.

The victory and the hero were not soon forgotten. With the passage of time and the zeal of patriotic promoters, George Croghan underwent a minor apotheosis. In 1835, Congress authorized the striking of a gold medal in his honor. It was more than twenty years after the event, but the Senate oratory in praise of Croghan was not dimmed by the years. Senator George M. Bibb, of Kentucky, who introduced the resolution in the Senate, spoke of the defense of the fort as "the cause of saving all the Western country from the hostile and destructive incursion of the British and Indians." With all the rhetoric at his command he called to mind that "Colonel Croghan might, without any dishonor, have preferred a course safer, indeed, to himself, but disastrous to his country, by not persevering in a defence which appeared so difficult, nay, so impossible, that to have abandoned the fort, to have left the West open to the enemy, would have been deemed a necessary, a prudent, and not a pusillanimous proceeding; yet, in the face of every obstacle, under the weight of every discouragement, he, with a handful of brave men, presented a bold and undaunted front to the enemy, arrested them on the threshold of the West, and saved Ohio and the adjoining states from invasion, from desolation, from plunder, and from bloodshed."[5]

In 1839 began a series of formal celebrations marking the anniversary of the victory of Fort Stephenson. In 1852, "Old Betsy" or "Good Bess," the single cannon used in the defense of the fort, was brought back to the original site; in

[5] The remarks of Senator Bibb are recorded in Gales and Seaton's *Debates in Congress*, XI, part 1 (1834–35), column 236. For debate in the House of Representatives, see *ibid.,* column 1093. The Resolution awarding the medal is in *United States Statutes at Large,* IV, 792. J. F. Loubat, *The Medallic History of the United States of America, 1776–1876* (New York, 1878) gives a description of the medal.

1860, Cassius M. Clay was the orator; and in 1885 a monument was unveiled in the presence of the President of the United States and other distinguished guests. An even greater day was the celebration of 1906, when the remains of Croghan, discovered after a long search in the family burial plot at Locust Grove, Kentucky, were brought in state to Fremont and reinterred at the base of the monument. A mammoth affair planned for the one-hundredth anniversary, August 2, 1913, had to be limited in its scope because of the destruction caused by floods in the river valley. Such was the tribute paid by a grateful nation to a deserving hero.[6]

After Lower Sandusky, Croghan served ably at Detroit and on the upper lakes and then in New Orleans at the close of the war. In 1817, however, he resigned his commission, perhaps because of his irritation at not being promoted to full colonel and because of general dissatisfaction with the promotion system in the army.[7] A year earlier he had married Serena Livingston, daughter of John R. Livingston, of New York, and a niece of Chancellor Robert Livingston. They moved to New Orleans, where her uncle, Edward Livingston, was a prominent citizen. In 1824, Croghan was postmaster of New Orleans, but he soon reappeared as Colonel Croghan, one of the two inspectors general of the army, to begin the long period of devoted and unostentatious service with which we are concerned.

At the death of Inspector General Samuel B. Archer in

[6] These celebrations are described in Lucy Elliot Keeler, "The Croghan Celebration," *Ohio Archaeological and Historical Publications,* Vol. XVI (1907), 1–112, and Lucy Elliot Keeler, "The Centennial of Croghan's Victory," *ibid.,* Vol. XXII (1914), 1–33.

[7] See George Croghan to General Andrew Jackson, October 14, 1815, and Memorial to the President and Senate from Officers of the 8th Military Department (enclosure in letter of February 2, 1816), in Croghan Family Papers, Library of Congress.

1825, Croghan was recommended for the vacancy by important and influential men.[8] His old commander, William Henry Harrison, wrote to the Secretary of War: "If distinguished and important services are to form the criterion in making the selection for this office, I am persuaded that there is no person of his grade in the late army who can enter into competition with him." And seven members of the Senate and House stepped in on his behalf, insisting to Secretary of War Barbour that "the distinguished services of Colonel Croghan in the late war present the strongest claims to the consideration of the President and they equally prove him well qualified for this military appointment." These eminent men did not speak in vain, and on December 21, 1825, Croghan was appointed to the post. He felt awkward, he wrote to his brother-in-law, for he had "not looked at a military book in 10 years."[9]

[8] Croghan's family had been interested in some sort of federal appointment for him in recognition of his services during the war, and there was talk of an appointment to Mexico. Croghan then got the postmastership of New Orleans, but he was not happy in that city, and his eyes turned back to the army when Inspector General Archer died. See John Croghan to General Thomas Jesup, February 25, 1823, and George Croghan to Jesup, August 19, 1825, in Croghan Family Papers, Library of Congress.

[9] William Henry Harrison to Secretary of War James Barbour, December 14, 1825, and John Rowan and others to Barbour, December 14, 1825, in Letters Received 1826 (C 105), Adjutant General's Office, National Archives; Orders 88, Adjutant General's Office, December 31, 1825.

Croghan's views on his appointment are expressed in a letter to his brother-in-law, General Jesup: "Mr. Clay, General Harrison, Colonel Johnston and you (more especially) are entitled to and shall receive on the first opportunity that may occur, my personal expression of grateful thanks, for the active part you have taken in obtaining for me the place in question.

"I take for granted that my course will be *severely* scrutinized for the first year or two especially by those who[se] feelings are *directly* wounded by my appointment from the rank of citizens. But run and remark as they may, no *causes* of regret will ever visit those who have shown themselves my friends. I will of course be a little awkward at first (for I have not looked at a military book in 10 years), yet I have not a fear about my becoming very soon all that once might have been." Croghan to Jesup, February 7, 1826, Croghan Family Papers, Library of Congress.

In the following May he received his first assignment in the West, to inspect the posts on the upper Mississippi and Missouri rivers.[10]

The scope and excellence of the inspections will appear from the selections printed in this book. It was routine work, and no mention of this service intrudes into the celebrations of the 1813 victory. Undoubtedly it was more pleasant to look back to the past glory of Fort Stephenson than to examine too closely the humdrum present. And in his later years as inspector general, Croghan was under something of a cloud. The main trouble was drink, an affliction which did not accord well with the prestige and dignity of an inspector general and which was a severe cross to his family. So many ill reports floated in to General Alexander Macomb that he set about to investigate. Macomb inquired especially of Brigadier General John E. Wool, first inspector general, who submitted a far from favorable report. It would appear, however, that Croghan reformed to some extent, and General Edmund P. Gaines interceded for him with the Secretary of War. In the end, no disciplinary action was taken, and he went on his customary rounds inspecting the western posts.[11]

George Croghan had almost constant financial difficulties, and his pay vouchers were often pledged to creditors. In 1845, when a crisis arose from serious mismanagement of his ac-

[10] Special Orders 67, Adjutant General's Office, May 17, 1826.

[11] Alexander Macomb to John E. Wool, February 20, 1841, in Private and Confidential Letters of General Macomb, Headquarters of the Army, National Archives; Wool to Macomb, February 22, 1841, and Macomb to Secretary of War Joel R. Poinsett, February 23, 1841, in Joel R. Poinsett Papers, volume 16, Historical Society of Pennsylvania; Croghan to Secretary of War J. C. Spencer, April 6, 1842, in Letters Received 1845 (C 163), Adjutant General's Office, National Archives. For examples of the disturbance in Croghan's family over his intemperance, see John Croghan to Thomas Jesup, April 9, 1835, and William Croghan to Jesup, May 8, 1835, in Croghan Family Papers, Library of Congress.

counts, he was charged with having illegally received double payment. Formal charges and specifications were drawn up and a court martial appointed. Croghan submitted a letter of explanation, in which he sought to exonerate himself. Finally, after an exchange of correspondence between the Secretary of War, the Adjutant General, the Paymaster General, and the President, the charges were canceled by President Polk and the court martial never met.[12]

When the Mexican War brought a new phase of activity for the army, Croghan's efforts were turned in that direction. He mustered in troops and took an active part in the war himself with the army under General Zachary Taylor. It was not a happy time. He was ill, dropping from 168 to 148 pounds in weight in the two weeks after arriving at Monterrey, and he was worried by the financial problems in the family estate. He expressed great eagerness to leave Mexico.[13]

At the end of the war he returned briefly to Locust Grove and then to New Orleans, where he died of cholera on January 8, 1849.

Croghan's position as inspector general made him an essential and important cog in the administration of the army, but it would be a mistake to transpose to Croghan's time the sort of inspector general staff and organization with which we are familiar in the modern army. Just as the army itself was

[12] The bulk of official documents relating to Croghan's pay difficulties are found in a bundle in Letters Received 1845 (C 162), Adjutant General's Office, National Archives. See also General Orders No. 16, Adjutant General's Office, April 30, 1845; Roger Jones to Croghan, May 19, May 24, and May 27, 1845, in Letters Sent, volume 21, Adjutant General's Office; Croghan to Secretary of War William L. Marcy, May 24, 1845, in Letters Received 1845 (C 166), Adjutant General's Office. The Croghan Family Papers, Library of Congress, contain many letters relating to Croghan's financial troubles.

[13] George Croghan to John Croghan, October 5, 1847, in Croghan Family Papers, Library of Congress.

small in size and simple in organization, so too was the inspection routine. There was no distinct Inspector General's Department, in fact, until after the Civil War. In the Revolutionary War the inspector general was an individual attached to an army headquarters without an official staff of his own. When the General Staff was organized in 1816, provision was made for one adjutant and inspector general of the army, with rank of brigadier general, one inspector general for each division, with rank of colonel, and an assistant for each brigade, taken from the line. When the army was reduced in 1821, the inspecting duties fell upon two inspectors general, each with the rank of colonel.[14] It was under this arrangement that Croghan was appointed to the post of inspector general in 1825. John E. Wool, who had been appointed an inspector general in 1816, continued to serve in that capacity until 1841. Wool regularly inspected the artillery fortifications along the coast, leaving for Croghan the more arduous and difficult tour of the western frontier.

The actual assignment of posts to be inspected in any given tour as well as the exact time of departure were matters which were ironed out between the General-in-chief and Croghan as each year rolled around. As a rule, headquarters called the tune, and Croghan's travels were outlined for him in a letter or an order from his superior, directing him when to proceed, what general route to follow, and what posts to visit.[15] But

[14] A brief history of the Inspector General's Department with extracts of pertinent laws can be found in Raphael P. Thian, *Legislative History of the General Staff of the Army of the United States* (Washington, 1901), 83–118, and Thomas H. S. Hamersly, *Complete General Army Register of the United States of America from the Time of the Revolutionary War to the Present Time* (New York, 1888), part 2, 269–72.

[15] For examples see Orders 16, Adjutant General's Office, March 21, 1827; Macomb to Croghan, March 23, 1830, May 14, 1831, and June 14, 1834, in Letter Books, volumes 1 and 2, Headquarters of the Army, National Archives.

a good deal of leeway was always allowed, and Croghan's own advice or desires were heeded. In 1830 and 1832, in fact, because of sickness in his family, he kept begging postponement of his departure until it was too late to proceed at all, and he made no tour of the West in those years.[16]

The inspection reports which Croghan submitted to Washington followed a set form. Were it not for Croghan's frank observations and sharp style and for his frequent appended "remarks," in which he departed from the stereotyped form imposed by regulations, the reports would be extremely monotonous. The regulations demanded that a report be submitted for each establishment—military post, arsenal, or armory—and further demanded that the inspectors general "report separately under the heads pointed out in these regulations, and not blend the whole together, with one general remark. Each inspection-report should be complete in itself, and contain a full and faithful representation, with such suggestions as they may consider necessary for the improvement of all the objects to which their attention may be directed."[17]

A stickler for form, Croghan seldom departed from the prescribed manner of reporting. Each report was divided into a series of paragraphs, according to the object being inspected. Titles which uniformly appear are administration, men's messing, service, instruction, discipline, hospital and medical stores, ordnance, quartermaster department, subsistence department, arms and equipments, bunks and arms racks, and books. The actual format, although covering items re-

---

[16] Croghan to Macomb, August 6, 1830, July 17, and August 17, 1832, in Document File, Headquarters of the Army, National Archives; Macomb to Croghan, July 11, 1832, in Letter Book, volume 2, Headquarters of the Army.

[17] The various editions of *General Regulations for the Army* included special articles devoted to the inspector's department. See especially Article 77 in the *Regulations* for 1825 and Article 73 in the edition of 1841.

quired by the official documents, was quite likely of Croghan's own doing, since early in his career he had been informed by the Adjutant General that the annual reports were generally "constructed according to the dictate of the Inspector General himself."[18]

From time to time the General-in-chief sent specific instructions to Croghan, augmenting the details set forth in the *General Regulations for the Army*. These instructions were welcomed by Croghan as a more exact indication of what was expected of him in his tours of inspection. Particularly detailed was the letter of May 16, 1829, which General Alexander Macomb addressed to both Wool and Croghan. He directed them to check on the duties of officers, noncommissioned officers, and privates as pointed out by regulations and then added to this general admonition a set of special paragraphs which became a standard reference for Croghan. Macomb prefaced the instructions with a statement of his motive: "Yet as I am desirous of being well informed, on every subject connected with the military service, the character of the officers, and the several regiments, detachments and even individuals composing the Military Peace establishment, both as to their merits and demerits, I should naturally look to the Inspector General for particular and minute information on all the subjects connected with these considerations, and for a full disclosure of everything which ought to be known to the General in Chief of an Army. . . ."

Then followed the points he wanted inspected with special care. Since they give an admirable picture of the general scope of Croghan's work on the frontier, we will do well to consider them here in their entirety:

[18] Roger Jones to Croghan, October 3, 1826, in Letters Sent, volume 7, Adjutant General's Office, National Archives.

1st. To the general distribution of the troops, whether under the circumstances of defence, of accommodation, of comfort, of health and of economy they are well posted: if not, what changes you would recommend.

2nd. The quantity of Ordnance and Ordnance supplies necessary at each station, for its defence, and for practical instruction, and the respectability of the posts, whether occupied by Artillery or Infantry.

3d. Distribution of the Arsenals and Depots under the direction of the Ordnance, whether such distribution is most judicious and what new depots if any are required.

4th. The regulations now in force, if requiring any alteration, whether any part is useless or of no effect and ou[gh]t to be stricken out of the book, and new regulations under the different heads inserted. These remarks may be made with reference to the paragraphs and articles to which they may appertain.

5th. The General Orders issued from General Headquarters, War Department, or Department Head Quarters, if obeyed; if you discover any thing in any of these orders producing a good effect, to so state, if on the contrary be particular in noting the defects and effects.

6th. The Articles of War, if they can be improved and in what particular.

7th. Under the head of discipline, give your opinion on the effects produced on the discipline of the Army by the abolishing of corporeal punishment by stripes or lashes.

8th. The Rations—state your opinion of the component parts, whether well apportioned, if there be too much or too little of any of the articles, if any should be dispensed with and others substituted, especially whether the liquor be injurious to the health or not.

9th. The clothing, as to quality and quantity: whether the dress could not be improved—state your ideas in full.

It is desirable that your report should be furnished in time for the annual report of the Army which will be made in the early part of November.[19]

The written reports submitted to Washington are uniform in style but vary somewhat in length. They are written on folded sheets of paper in a close hand. An average report for the tour of the western posts runs to about forty pages. Occasionally, when special extensive remarks are added, the bulk swells considerably, but in some years only the barest outline was submitted. Croghan admitted some difficulty in keeping his notes together and frequently was delayed in completing his final draft because trunks containing his inspection notes had not yet caught up with him in his travels. Travel conditions were by no means ideal in the primitive West, and Croghan cannot be severely censured, but one is tempted to suspect that his habits of intemperance did not aid in keeping his notes in good order and always conveniently at hand.

Croghan was officially a part of the general staff, but he

[19] Alexander Macomb to John E. Wool and Croghan, May 16, 1829, in Letter Book, volume 1, Headquarters of the Army, National Archives. Croghan replied to Macomb from Louisville, June 13, 1829:

"I would beg leave to express my gratification upon the receipt yesterday of your communication of the 16th May and to offer you every assurance that your instructions therein contained shall be complied with to the full extent of my ability.

"My reports hitherto have not been so full and satisfactory I fear as the General in Chief might have expected or desired; but to anything rather than carelessness on my part let this be ascribed. Having no guide other than the book of General Regulations to direct me in the course of my inspection, I have as of course often neglected to examine many points of paramount consideration, but this cannot again occur, now that I have set before me all the objects towards which the General in Chief would call my particular attention." Document File, Headquarters of the Army, National Archives.

seems to have had no set office or duties in the capital. His work was out on tour, and his place of abode did not greatly matter. He lived some of the time in New York, moved to Georgetown, then begged leave to set up his home on the Hudson River, near his father-in-law. Much of his official correspondence is dated from these spots.

We must conclude that Croghan was a lone operator most of the time and was not burdened with a large staff of subordinates. His paper work was of the simplest sort. At each post he took notes on the various departments and phases of army life which he inspected. These notes might be written up in final form at the completion of each post inspection, but the report which he forwarded to the General-in-chief was written (or at least transcribed from the original reports) at the end of each year's tour. For this work and for necessary correspondence and bookkeeping, Croghan at times had the aid of a secretary. Some of the final reports, however, are in Croghan's own hand.

The inspectors general were the eyes and ears of the General-in-chief. There is no doubt that a good deal of the efficient operation and improvement in the army depended upon their careful observations and frank comments. In Croghan the army had an accomplished soldier and a man whose love of things military made him an admirable watchdog for correct instruction and military discipline. Recommendations which he made found their way into War Department orders and into the new editions of the *General Regulations*. His long term of service indicates that he was respected despite his aberrations, yet he was not always able to exert the influence he desired. There were many forces at work, political as well as military, upon the organization and life of the army over which Croghan had no control. That sometimes he seems like a voice crying out with conviction and earnestness, yet little heard or heeded, does not detract from the value his reports have as a picture of army life on the western frontier.

WESTERN POSTS
INSPECTED BY CROGHAN

FORT ARMSTRONG was established in 1816 on the southern end of Rock Island in the Mississippi as part of the advance of American authority into the upper Mississippi Valley after the War of 1812. Croghan inspected the fort in 1826, 1827, 1831, and 1834. The fort was abandoned in 1836.

FORT ATKINSON (Iowa), a Dragoon post on the Turkey River in the northeast corner of Iowa, was established in 1840 in order to control the Winnebago Indians, who were moved to a reservation in Iowa in that year. It was abandoned in 1849, after the Winnebagoes were removed to Minnesota. Croghan inspected Fort Atkinson in 1840, 1842, 1843, and 1845.

FORT ATKINSON (Nebraska) was founded in 1819 as a result of a large movement of troops up the Missouri under General Henry Atkinson. The post was located on the right bank of the Missouri, near the present city of Omaha. In 1827 the fort was abandoned, its troops being transferred to Jefferson Barracks. Croghan inspected the post on his first western tour (1826).

BATON ROUGE BARRACKS was established in 1820, and the city was regularly a center for concentration of American troops.

An arsenal was established there in 1826. Croghan inspected the troops at Baton Rouge in 1827 and 1829 and again in 1844.

FORT BRADY was established at Sault Ste Marie in 1822 and served as a key outpost in the northwestern chain of defense until its abandonment at the time of the Mexican War. Croghan visited this post frequently as he toured the lakes on his way to or from the Mississippi: 1826, 1827, 1831, 1834, 1838, 1842, 1843, and 1845.

FORT CRAWFORD was established in 1816 at a strategic point in the West, near the confluence of the Wisconsin and Mississippi rivers at Prairie du Chien, Wisconsin. The post was temporarily abandoned in 1826 and regarrisoned the following year because of Indian disturbances. A new post was started in 1829 and was steadily occupied until 1845, when the regular army troops were dispatched to Texas. Croghan inspected Fort Crawford in 1826, 1831, 1833, 1834, 1836, 1838, 1840, 1842, 1843, and 1845.

FORT DES MOINES (No. 1), a temporary camp established in 1834 on the western bank of the Mississippi, was located at the site of the present town of Montrose, Iowa. Its purpose was to control the Sacs and Foxes and to prevent encroachment on the Indian lands by whites. Croghan inspected the post twice, in 1835 and 1836, before its abandonment in the summer of 1837.

FORT DES MOINES (No. 2) was a Dragoon post founded in 1843 at the Raccoon Fork of the Des Moines River, at the present city of Des Moines. The purpose of the garrison was to prevent whites from overrunning the lands of the Indians until the red men had withdrawn according to treaty. The fort was abandoned in 1846. Croghan had inspected it only once, in 1845.

DETROIT BARRACKS was established in 1838 and abandoned in 1851. An arsenal, at Dearbornville, was founded in 1832. Croghan inspected these establishments in 1838, 1842, 1843, and 1845.

FORT GIBSON was built in 1824 in what is now the state of Oklahoma, on the left bank of the Neosho or Grand River, two and one-half miles from its confluence with the Arkansas. It protected settlement advancing along the Red and Arkansas rivers and was an important outpost in the Indian Territory for many years. Croghan inspected the post in 1827 and again in 1844.

FORT GRATIOT was located on the western shore of the St. Clair River in 1814, in order to control the entrance to Lake Huron. It was abandoned in 1822, with the establishment of Fort Brady. When a new disposition of forces on the northwest frontier was made in 1828, the post was reoccupied. Croghan inspected the post on his tours of the lakes in 1833, 1838, 1842, 1843, 1845.

FORT HOWARD was established in 1816 at the mouth of the Fox River, now in the city of Green Bay, Wisconsin, as a key point in the route of communication between the Great Lakes and the Mississippi. It was abandoned in 1841, then briefly reoccupied from 1849 to 1852. Croghan inspected the fort in 1826, 1828, 1831, 1833, 1834, and 1838.

FORT JACKSON was a coastal defense located on the west bank

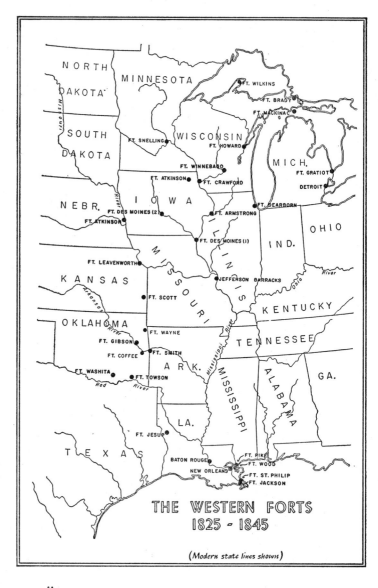

THE WESTERN FORTS
1825 - 1845

(Modern state lines shown)

of the Mississippi sixty-five miles below New Orleans. Construction of the post commenced in 1814. Croghan visited the fort during his tour of 1827.

JEFFERSON BARRACKS was located on the west bank of the Mississippi a short distance below St. Louis. It was established in 1826 and long remained a key concentration for troops in the Mississippi Valley. The fort was regularly inspected and was included in Croghan's tours of 1827, 1829, 1831, 1833, 1834, 1840, 1842, 1843, and 1844.

FORT JESUP was established in 1822 in western Louisiana, on the ridge dividing the waters of the Red River from those of the Sabine, as part of the movement of troops into the Southwest for Indian control. The fort, which had been part of Croghan's tour in 1827, 1829, and 1844, was abandoned during the Mexican War.

FORT LEAVENWORTH filled the need for a post to provide security in the region west of Missouri and protection for the Santa Fé trade. The post was established in 1827 on the west bank of the Missouri River near the mouth of the Little Platte; it became an important Dragoon post after the authorization of the Dragoon regiment in 1833. The post was inspected by Croghan nine times—in 1829, 1831, 1834, 1836, 1838, 1840, 1842, 1843, and 1844.

FORT MACKINAC was located on a bluff on the southeastern part of the island of Mackinac, between Lakes Michigan and Huron. The fort was returned to the United States at the end of the war of 1812. Croghan inspected the post in 1826, 1828, 1831, 1833, 1834, 1838, 1842, 1843, and 1845.

NEW ORLEANS BARRACKS was erected in 1834 and 1835 on the east bank of the Mississippi just below New Orleans, although troops had been stationed in the city at earlier times. Croghan inspected here in 1827 and again in 1844.

FORT PIKE, located on the northern margin of Petites Coquilles Island, about thirty-five miles northeast of New Orleans, was begun in 1819. Croghan inspected the fort in 1829 and 1844.

ST. LOUIS ARSENAL was established in 1827. Croghan inspected it in 1840, 1842, and 1844.

FORT ST. PHILIP was built on the east bank of the Mississippi, opposite and a short distance above Fort Jackson. It was on the site of an installation built by the Spaniards in the middle of the eighteenth century. Croghan visited the post in 1827 and 1829.

FORT SCOTT was located in Kansas, four miles west of the Missouri state line. The fort was established in 1842 as part of the cordon of western defense and was visited by Croghan in 1844. It was abandoned as a military post during 1853 and 1854.

FORT SMITH was established in 1817 as part of the original American military barrier in the Southwest. It was built on the south bank of the Arkansas River, at the western limit of the state of Arkansas. Abandoned in 1824 and reoccupied in 1827, it served as a military post until after the Civil War. Croghan inspected it only once, in his tour of 1844.

FORT SNELLING was established in 1819 as the United States

began to exert its authority in the upper Mississippi Valley after the War of 1812. The post was built on the bluff overlooking the confluence of the Minnesota and Mississippi rivers and served as a key frontier post until 1858. Croghan visited the fort in 1827, 1831, 1834, 1836, 1838, 1840, 1842, 1843, and 1845.

FORT TOWSON was established in 1824 in the Choctaw Nation, a few miles north of the Red River and fifty miles west of the Arkansas boundary. Because of the expense of maintaining the post, it was abandoned in 1829. It was reoccupied in 1831 on account of Indian troubles and then garrisoned until 1854. Croghan included it in his tours of 1827 and 1844.

FORT WASHITA was built in 1842 on the Washita River in Oklahoma, near its confluence with the Red River, and served as a military post until 1861. Croghan visited the post in 1844.

FORT WINNEBAGO was established in 1828 at the portage between the Fox and Wisconsin rivers (at present-day Portage, Wisconsin). The post served as an important link in the chain of western defense until the removal of the Winnebagoes and was abandoned in 1845. Croghan visited the fort in 1831, 1833, 1834, 1838, 1843, and 1845.

FORT WOOD was built on the right bank of Chef Menteur Pass, twenty-five miles from New Orleans, to command the passage into Lake Ponchartrain. It was erected between 1825 and 1827 and was inspected by Croghan in 1829 and 1844.

Note: In some years Croghan, on his return trip from the

western forts, inspected also the posts along the northern frontier in New York state: Buffalo Barracks, Fort Niagara, Fort Ontario, Madison Barracks, and Plattsburg Barracks. He visited one or more of these posts in 1831, 1838, 1843, and 1845.

ARMY LIFE ON THE WESTERN FRONTIER

1: MILITARY POLICY

O NE OF the Inspector General's chief responsibilities was to
report to the General-in-chief on the strategic location of
the army troops assigned to the West. How best to distribute
the soldiers was a problem of special concern in an army of
small size and large duties. Croghan obviously delighted in this
part of his task. He had had considerable military experience
and did not lack self-assurance when it came to setting forth
his own ideas of what was best for the defense of the frontier.
Not only did he repeatedly criticize the locations and the fortifications of the posts, but he was constantly on the alert to catch
anything which might be considered a deviation from the strict
military spirit which his training and temperament had made a
part of him.

At the end of his first inspection tour—that of 1826—Croghan appended a long section to his report, blasting the unmili-
tariness of the posts he had visited. It was perhaps a natural
reaction for a man whose last military service had been in the
heat of war and who now faced the life of the peacetime army,
when things military often seemed to have been relegated to
second place. Contempt for the soldier-turned-farmer flows from
his pen, and posts not instantly ready for attack are sharply
rebuked.

In 1833, Croghan added to his regular inspection report a
general survey of the military frontier in the West, from Sault
Ste Marie to New Orleans, in which he gave an admirable pic-

3

ture of the state of the western frontier on a post-by-post basis.[1] This long report and the shorter selections of this first chapter set the stage for the more particularized items which caught the attention of the Inspector General and which he in turn passed on to the officials of the army in Washington.

St. Louis, October, 1826

Having now completed an inspection of the posts designated in the order of 17th May, 1826, from General Headquarters, I will proceed to make some general remarks which could not have been previously so well introduced.[2] I certainly might and would have passed by without notice the misnomer of fort as applied to the post at Sault Ste Marie [Fort Brady], in my inspection of that place, had I been informed of the true character of the forts along the lines which I have since visited, for it is very nearly as well entitled to its present appellation as Fort Howard, as equally as Fort Crawford, and far more so than Fort Atkinson, which in itself presents the best defence possible against—not the Indians, but the attacks of those who would deprive them of all merit of good faith and common honesty, for they have made no attempts upon the fort although it is indefensible, have in no instance slaughtered or driven off any of the cattle, which roam about in hundreds on the plains, oftentimes without a guard, have never pillaged any of the store houses, commissaries, quartermasters or ordnance, although they are all

[1] For basic data about the military posts which Croghan visited in the West, see pages *xxix–xxxvi*.

[2] Special Orders 67, Adjutant General's Office, May 17, 1826, outlined Croghan's tour in the most general terms: "Colonel Croghan will inspect the posts on the upper Mississippi and Missouri and will pursue his route by way of the Lakes." For a list of posts visited by Croghan in each year he inspected, see Appendix, pages 175–80.

4

without the square enclosed by the lines of barracks and easily to be entered by those disposed to pillage.

Fort Atkinson is certainly the weakest, and Fort Snelling the strongest work which I have visited, but all of them are objectionable from their great extent. Fort Armstrong is the least so, and it is too large by one half for its present garrison of two companies. Our frontier posts ought to be viewed as if placed directly upon the lines of a hostile territory and should therefore be prepared for immediate hostilities. The posts should be strong in themselves, the garrison sufficient, well supplied, and throughout that vigilant police observed which would presuppose a state of war. This is far from being the case; it would seem that the purpose was not to operate upon the fears of the Indians by an array of military strength and an appearance of constant watchfulness, but to gain them over by the softer arguments of unreserved intercourse and unsuspecting confidence. I now repeat that which I before asserted, "Our military have lost character among the Indians," and that it can not be recovered under a continuance of the present system of external police.

Ask an officer at one of those posts what his place is in the event of alarms, and his answer will be, I don't know, no particular one has been assigned to me; we never have alarms, either false or real. Direct the officer in command to receive an enemy that will attack him in a few minutes, and it will be found that he requires half a day of preparation. He has to designate the different stations, to appoint to those particular commands and after all to set an enquiry on foot as to the best men to place at the guns before he can discharge a single piece. Order a shell to be thrown, and the time for firing three or more will be taken up in finding one small enough to enter the muzzle of the howitzer, as was the case at Fort Snelling.

That the Indians are at peace and that nothing is likely to disturb the present quiet argues not at all against the positive necessity for placing our frontiers in a position the best calculated to invite military criticism. As well might the propriety of entirely disbanding the army be urged upon us for the same reason, and truly, I would advocate the latter, sooner than witness a total annihilation of all military feeling under the operations of the present system, a system which would sink the proud soldier into the menial and reduce him who may have gallantly led in the front of our enemies into the base overseer of a troop of awkward ploughmen.

Let the soldier return to himself, let him no longer be permitted to boast of his success as a tiller of the soil but be encouraged to pride himself on his advancement in the knowledge of the proud science of which he is an elected professor. He will not, he can not, be esteemed the worse citizen from being the more accomplished soldier. I do not say that a soldier shall never be called upon to do duties, unless such as may advance him as a tactician—far from it. I wish him to be occupied and desire only that such service as he may be called to perform, not purely military, may be considered as secondary. I would have the soldier point to his garden in proof of the good provision he has made during the short intervals from military exercise, rather than boastingly talk of his proficiency as a farmer, of the advantages of the *broadcast* over the *drill,* or of the five bushels of corn per acre made by Company C more than by Company B from relying more upon the plough than upon the hoe.

What has been gained by this anti-military course to compensate for the great loss of moral strength which has been sustained? Nothing, so far as I have been enabled to ascertain, that is of true value to the soldier. A few dollars may

6

have been added to the administrative fund, but at what a cost! Look at Fort Atkinson and you will see barn yards that would not disgrace a Pennsylvania farmer, herds of cattle that would do credit to a Potomac grazier, yet where is the gain in this, either to the soldier or to the government? Ask the individual who boastingly shews you all this, why such a provision of hay and corn. His answer will be, to *feed* the cattle. But why so many *cattle?* Why—to eat the *hay and corn.*

In saying so much against this system of citizen soldier making, I intend not a word against any officer for his want of proper external police. His excuse can be found in the operation of circumstances, over the enervating influence of which he has had no control. If asked whether or not under a different administration of external police the frontier line of which Sault Ste Marie is the right could be considered as safe in a military point of view, I would unhesitatingly say it could not, the distribution of the troops being in itself bad and the works occupied throughout indefensible. Should any of the posts be threatened, where is the disposable force to send to its relief. There is none, and if there were, there is no responsible head to direct it within twenty days. Colonel [Josiah] Snelling of the 5th Regiment, commanding at St. Peters [Fort Snelling], is but the officer of a post, and General [Hugh] Brady, who commands at Green Bay [Fort Howard], is in the same restrained situation.

Neither has the least control over the commandants of the posts in his vicinity, although they be captains of his own regiment. Each has his regiment and each is considered as responsible for its character in the public eye at least, and yet neither is permitted to make visits of inspection or to enquire into the conduct of the detached companies of his regiment. If I have not forgot the language of the order,

7

Colonel Snelling has been severely reprimanded for presuming to make a change in the garrison of a post in his vicinity when circumstances, in his opinion, rendered it necessary that he should assume the responsibility. Colonels of artillery are, we find, not only permitted but positively instructed to make frequent visits of inspection to the artillery posts. Why, I would respectfully ask, this degrading distinction, this unequal distribution of favors, to the prejudice of equally gallant officers who have long suffered and are still suffering under this indirect imputation of their being unworthy of equal confidence with those of other corps?

If the 5th Regiment be left on the Mississippi, Colonel Snelling should reoccupy Prairie du Chien and establish there his headquarters and should place garrisons of one company each at St. Peters, the portage of the Ouisconsin, and at Rock Island.[3] On the lake quarter, let the nine companies of the 2nd be given—two to Sault Ste Marie, one to Mackinac, and the remaining six companies be left with General Brady at his headquarters, Green Bay. The works at the several places occupied should be of sufficient strength, not too large for defence by a small force and yet capable of receiving on an emergency any necessary increase to their garrison. From such a distribution there could be furnished at any moment eleven disposable companies to march in any required direction, and this without weakening any particular part of the line, for the disposable companies form not, either at Green Bay or at Prairie du Chien, a portion of the proper garrison

[3] Fort Crawford at Prairie du Chien had been evacuated in 1826. Indian disturbances, however, soon necessitated its reoccupation and troops returned in 1827. Fort Snelling, at the confluence of the St. Peters (Minnesota) River and the Mississippi, and Fort Armstrong at Rock Island were important links in the early chain of western defenses. The post urged by Croghan for the portage of the Wisconsin was established in 1828 and named Fort Winnebago.

of the post but are cantoned without the walls, near enough to be under proper cover of the guns. These disposable companies might be kept in constant and profitable employment. Detachments could be frequently sent (properly equipped as frontier soldiers) to visit the various Indian towns—much practice may be had in field engineering, and should it be thought necessary, the five companies from Green Bay might meet the six companies from Prairie du Chien at the post of the Ouisconsin for the purpose of such military exercise as they might be least conversant in. Such movements might be made without one additional cent of cost to the government, to the great advantage of the soldier, and to the equally great additional security of the frontier.[4]

Fort Jackson, June, 1827

I have not conversed with any of our engineers in relation to this fortress [and], of course, have not been set aright. I must therefore be permitted to enjoy and to express my

---

[4] While at St. Louis near the close of his first tour, Croghan wrote to his brother-in-law: "I reached this place from St. Peters about the first of this month and would at this time be at or near the [Council] Bluffs but that I was taken sick of fever which confined me for a week to my bed and a longer time to the house. I have pretty nearly recovered my strength and having a good appetite will be myself again before I reach the confines of the state. I can not say that my tour thus far has been a pleasant one. I have been much exposed to the influences of the weather and almost throughout without a travelling companion. I have been interested, only though in as much as I passed through a wilderness country that I had never before seen. I have visited the posts on the lakes and the Mississippi and in the time have gained enough to satisfy me that the present disposition of the two Regiments which garrison them is as bad and ill judged as it could be— I am wrong, it will be worse when the post at Prairie du Chien is broken up and its garrison removed to St. Peters. Who in name of all that is military, could have advised General Brown to direct the abandonment of Prairie du Chien, the *only* important military position on the upper Mississippi?" Croghan to Thomas Jesup, September 21, 1826, Croghan Family Papers, Library of Congress.

9

opinion, which I do most candidly (although it be contradictory of the generally received one) when I assert that one half of the money already spent towards its erection would complete a work sufficiently strong for such a location. If the government funds must be disbursed in this quarter, let more of them be appropriated to the defences of St. Philip. Mount a hundred guns on the ramparts of Fort Jackson, if you will; still in the event of trial it will be found that most of the effective shots are fired from the few pieces pointed from St. Philip.

Fort Jesup, July, 1827

Why a post has been established here, I am at a loss to conjecture. As a private residence it is desirable enough, being well watered and healthy, but as a military location it surely can boast of no other than these single advantages, which have hitherto not been considered of primary and exclusive importance. I may probably think differently after having consulted a good map of the country with the gentleman who first recommended the establishment of the post, but not until then.

Fort Leavenworth, March 31, 1829

Cantonment Leavenworth is full near enough to the settlements, and if it be abandoned as too sickly, let health be found somewhere further up. Advance, do not retrograde an inch if you wish for the quiet of the frontier. A position taken up a dozen miles from a navigable river would serve as a check upon the Indians as well as though it were upon the river itself, for it is not here as upon the upper Mississippi and its tributaries—there much use is made of the canoe; here one is never seen, the travelling is altogether by land.

Fort Jesup, May 3, 1829

There now no longer exists a necessity for my going further up the Red River. I will therefore retrace my steps to New Orleans, greatly relieved that I am saved from the fatigues of a very long ride, but still much disturbed by a dread of the probable consequences of the abandonment of Cantonment Towson. I am surely not at all informed as to the state of that frontier if every white family along it does not fall back upon the interior immediately upon the withdrawal of the troops. Of the propriety of this location I expressed a very positive opinion in my report upon two years ago. That opinion I still maintain unaltered and I believe without the least prospect of a change.

Baton Rouge, May 9, 1829

This place has more than once been left without a garrison, to the surprise of all who justly appreciated its importance. It is hoped that this will not again occur, and that it did ever occur must in charity be ascribed to ignorance on the part of him who caused it as to the situation of this country in relation to its slave population, and of the existence here of a large arsenal of military stores, the largest, in truth the only one with the exception of that at Pittsburgh, in the whole region watered by the Mississippi and its tributaries.

New Orleans needs not a garrison so much as many other places that could be named. It could protect itself if anything like a proper organization of its effective means were adopted (for the free citizens far outnumber the slave population), and the sooner the authorities of the city are told that for the future they must rely upon their own resources exclusively until they be found insufficient, the more immediately will they cease the cry of *help* which they have so often raised without the least effort on their part to help themselves. In this particular neighbourhood the black population far outnumbers the white, but no serious apprehensions need be presumed upon this circumstance either here or at any other point on the lower Mississippi. Partial outrages may be committed, it is true, and by the Negroes, but so long as the arsenal here is protected by a military force, a general rising or insurrection of them is out of the question. Negroes no more than whites can effect much without arms and ammunition, and until they do procure them, be assured that they will attempt nothing of a character so serious as to create alarms.

Washington, December 9, 1833

Having now completed my remarks upon the state and condition of the posts visited by me since August last, I will in the next place proceed to answer the queries which you have presented for my consideration, taking care to discuss them separately and in their proper order.[5]

1st. "The general distribution of the troops, whether under the circumstances of defence, of accommodation, of health and economy they are well posted."

To remarks upon the northwestern and southwestern frontiers I will confine myself in the consideration of this paragraph, as upon those alone I can speak with confidence and a knowledge derived from particular personal observation and inquiry. The seaboard, from New York to Eastport, has alone as yet come within the course of my inspection, and its defences when I last inspected them were in a most wretched

---

[5] In this chapter is included only the response to the first query, that concerning the distribution of troops. Answers to other questions in the same series will be found on pages 112–21.

condition, not a single post along the whole line, with the exception of Fort Independence perhaps, being able to protect itself against the insults of even an armed brig; if any of them had guns mounted, they were upon decayed carriages that could no longer traverse and upon platforms that had long before been declared unsafe.[6]

The northwestern and southwestern frontiers may be properly divided into two lines, the first reaching from the extreme right at Sault Ste Marie in a southwesterly direction to the Missouri River, and the second in a southerly direction to the Red and Mississippi rivers. How far the distribution of the posts along these lines is made with a just regard to military propriety as it may relate to their security against an enemy, I will first consider, and that I may be the better understood, I will remark upon each post separately and in its proper succession.

1st, Fort Brady. It would have been better had this post been located lower down the St. Marys River, at or near a place called "sailors' encampment," because by such a location the difficulties of an intricate navigation would have been avoided and that too without assuming in a military point of view a less eligible situation. I confess that the necessity for the occupancy of a point on the St. Marys has not as yet been made apparent to me, and why a garrison should be established at this particular place I am at a loss to conjecture, for in my judgment no substantial reasons can be assigned in support of its utility. This is no thoroughfare for Indians, nor has it ever been. The country round about offers no inducements to them; it furnishes but little game and is entirely unfit for tillage. Remove the Indian agency (which I would not advise) and but few Indians would be seen on the banks

[6] Croghan had inspected some of the seaboard posts in 1828.

of the St. Marys, unless during the fishing season or when on their annual route to Tenctanguishine to receive their customary presents from the British. If to keep in check the turbulent spirit of the Indians be the object of distributing troops along our frontier, that would be more effectually served by even a single company at the portage of the Fox and Ouisconsin rivers than by an entire regiment here.

It may be asked, shall the post be abandoned. I answer. A mistake has been committed; to endeavour to correct it by withdrawing the troops and abandoning the post would create quite a sensation in the village which has grown up since its establishment, for there would in that event be in prospect the certainty of an occasional outrage from the passing Indians, and the good people of the Sault Ste Marie, although but few in numbers, insist upon their having as strong a claim upon the protecting hand of the country as though they numbered an hundred thousand. How far these considerations should operate, it is not for me to determine.

Fort Mackinac. The occupancy of this point is important from the moral influence which it exerts over the lake and many of the Mississippi Indians. It is to them what Fort Niagara was of old to the Six Nations. The hand of fellowship is always extended to him of the *stone house,* be it a Fort Niagara or a Mackinac. An Indian's affections attach marvelously to those who are strong. The weak he despises and maltreats.

Fort Howard. This post, situate at the head of lake navigation and upon the long established route of communication with the Mississippi, is very properly garrisoned, and, from the facility with which troops may be dispatched to and from it and in any direction, it should be continued as the headquarters of the regiment or regiments serving on the upper lakes. It has besides a moral control over the Indians in this quarter of the country (derived from the fact of its having for a long time belonged first to the French and then to [the] English, of whom by a line of regular descent to the *strongest* we now rightfully hold) that has a greater agency in keeping them under restraint than could be obtained by the mere presence of troops unaided by this influence.

Fort Dearborn. Of the necessity for a garrison here I profess entire ignorance. The post I have never visited; of the number and disposition of the Indians still remaining in its neighbourhood I know but little and will therefore leave it to those better informed on the subject than I am to set forth reasons against the withdrawal of its garrison.

Fort Gratiot. This post was established by my order when I was in command of Detroit and its dependencies during the last war with Great Britain, to command the outlet of Lake Huron. During a state of war, and with that power, the position would be an important one, but how far that consideration should operate in determining the propriety of its occupancy in time of peace is a question that can be decided upon by others as well as by myself. I would, however, remark that, if its present occupancy have relation even to the most remote idea of a future rupture with Great Britain, a fortress of strength should forthwith be erected, but if our Indian neighbours are alone considered in the arrangement, then abandon it.

Fort Winnebago. It will be recollected that when I urged the immediate reoccupancy of Fort Crawford just after its abandonment in 1826 and twelve months before the Winnebago outrages, I expressed an opinion most decidedly in favor of the establishment of a post at this place, and in truth my surprise was great that so important a position should have been so long unnoticed.[7] The Winnebago Indians are now most completely in our power. We are, as it were, in the very heart of their country and so located with regard to navigation that a force may be embarked in an hour to strike at any hostile party, be it either on the waters of the lakes or those of the Mississippi. Not only have we secured to ourselves by the establishment of Fort Winnebago a safe communication between the lakes and the Mississippi along this important highway, but we have at the same time established a more respectable standing among the Indian tribes of this region of country, for in humbling the Winnebagoes, of whom they have all been for so long a time in dread, we have brought home to themselves a fuller knowledge of their really dependent condition.

Fort Crawford. No place upon our inland frontier is of more importance than this, and whether we view it in a physical or a moral point of view, its occupancy by our troops will be found to exercise a great control over the whole of the northwestern tribes of Indians. But with all its advantages of geographical position, its chief value to us as a military location is derived from the fact that like Mackinac it has for nearly a century been viewed by the Indians as the chosen spot of the strongest of their white fathers and the proper residence of his children, with whom it would be their best policy to keep upon terms of the most friendly kind. The expulsion of the British North West traders from our limits has also, like the occupancy of posts like this, the happiest influence and in truth tends more to the quiet of this frontier than all the show of military strength which we make along it. It speaks home to the Indians, telling them that their British Father, no longer strong, has been compelled to

[7] See the remarks of Croghan in his report of 1826, page 8.

yield his lands to the American Father, and that they must therefore be cautious how they offend the American, for in the event of their getting into trouble they must rely upon their own resources, as no aid can any longer be afforded to them.

Fort Snelling. The location of this post was made, I take it for granted, when it was the intention of the government to establish a cordon of posts at a greater distance from the settlements than the one at present occupied. I can in no other way account for its singularly isolated situation. I attach no importance to the post other than this indirect one, that by abandoning it the Indians might, in the excess of their vanity, be induced to ascribe the step to a conviction on our part of their superior strength and of our inability longer to hold the place, a blindness that might very soon lead them into trouble, an extremity which we should take care to prevent, if but in charity to them, for they are but tools in the hands of a few designing whites and half breeds, who take advantage of every backward movement of ours to flatter their vanity and thus to induce them to commit outrages upon us, seeking only gain to themselves, regardless of the consequences to the poor creatures whom they have deluded.

When Fort Crawford was abandoned in 1826, the tribes in its vicinity were easily induced to believe that it was caused by our apprehensions of an attack by them, and at the time a Sioux chief, to quiet our supposed fears, pledged himself to the late Colonel [Willoughby] Morgan that our troops might remain in perfect security where they were, as neither his band nor any other, as far as he could discover, had the least idea of molesting them. Had it not been abandoned, the Winnebago outrages in 1827 would not have been committed, and in all probability those subsequent discontents which eventu-

17

ated in the late Sauk War [Black Hawk War] would not have been created.

Fort Armstrong. The necessity for the continuance of a garrison at this place is much lessened since the terminating of the late Sauk War; indeed the post is at this moment of so little importance that I would recommend its abandonment in the course of the next summer and the occupancy in its stead of some point on the River Des Moines, say on the Raccoon Fork, at or near a place called Cedar Fort, a trading establishment of the North West Fur Company. The Indian agency too should in like manner be removed, for Rock Island is no longer within the Indian territory, and it is just as important that it should be in the very neighbourhood of the Indians as that our troops should be among them for the purpose of holding them in check and at the same time of protecting them against the frontier whites, who but seldom visit them for the single purpose of doing them a kindness.

Believe me, sir, that half the outrages committed by the Indians upon the whites are but in revenge for numerous ones committed by the whites upon them. The misfortune is that the Indians do not discriminate properly, and thus it is that the innocent sometimes suffer the punishment that might justly fall upon the guilty. In some of our early treaties with the Choctaws and other Indian tribes we find a clause inserted to the following effect: "If any citizen of the United States or other person not a citizen shall attempt to settle upon the Indian lands, such person shall forfeit the protection of the United States and the Indians may punish him or not as they please." A wise provision, and which were it now in force with respect to all Indians would very soon lessen the frequent hue and cry of outrages committed by them upon the settlements.

18

Fort Leavenworth. The occupancy of this point does not secure to us all the advantages that were derived from the establishment at Council Bluffs.[8] Nevertheless it forms an important link in the chain of posts (as may be seen on a reference to a map of the country) even without taking into consideration the circumstance of its location in the very neighbourhood of several tribes of Indians.

The Indians upon this southwestern frontier, of which this post may be said to form the extreme right, are not to be operated upon by those moral agencies which have been found to have effect over those of the northwestern and are only to be kept under control by the actual presence of a military force, so constituted as to convince them of its ability to punish at all times and promptly such as might dare to commit outrages, either upon our citizens or upon each other. It will prove no easy matter to hold in check the Indians lying between the Missouri and Arkansas rivers without the establishment of a post midway between the two, say on the Niosho River, at or near the village of the Osage chief, White Hair. The Pawnees are the deadly enemies of all the Indians along this line and especially of the Osages, with whom they are constantly at war, and in proportion as the Osages are pressed will they in turn trespass upon the whites and in self defence, for as they can neither protect their villages against attack nor hunt the buffalo without horses, they must seize upon the horses of the whites to supply the losses occasioned by the Pawnees.

During the occupancy of Council Bluffs we had it in our power to prevent the incursions of the Pawnees, for some of their villages being at no great distance, we had but to say to them, strike the Osages or any other Indians in the direc-

[8] Fort Atkinson, Nebraska, established in 1819 and abandoned in 1827.

tion of our settlements, and we will strike you, and they were afraid, but they no longer fear. They believe that, convinced of our weakness, we have shrunk back from their imposing strength, and they now act without dread of consequences from us and will continue so to do until the regiment of Dragoons now being organized shall prove to them that we have still power to punish those who deserve it at our hands.

Fort Gibson. This post would seem to have occupied at one time almost an exclusive importance, for while other posts were withdrawn, it remained, and for a season, the only one on the line from Prairie du Chien to Fort Jesup, a distance exceeding a 1,000 miles and through an Indian country. The post is, I agree, an important one, but be assured that much of its importance is derivative and that without some support from both the right and left it could not long remain in full consideration and would in the end be found to exercise but little influence, either over the Indians or the turbulent whites in its very neighbourhood.

Fort Towson. No point upon this frontier is of more importance than this, from the circumstance of its vicinity to the Texas boundary and its position with respect to the Indians on both sides of the line. Why its garrison was withdrawn in 1829 I know not, unless it was that the Indians who were scattered along the west side of the Red River above and below the Spanish bluffs when I last visited that country had located themselves . . . [beyond] the reach of its influence. Some assert that the abandonment of the place was caused by the too great expence of provisioning it. I am unwilling to credit this and am pretty sure that there is not a frontier man who would not feel indignant at the idea that his safety from the Indians was thus to be regulated and made dependent upon the cost of a loaf of bread. The question should never be, what will a ration cost at such a point, but rather, is the occupancy of that point calculated over any other to secure the repose and quiet of the frontier. In truth, no other can with any propriety be asked, so long as it is borne in mind that the integrity of the government is virtually pledged to the purchasers of public lands to secure them in the full possession and quiet enjoyment of them.

Fort Jesup. The advantages of this location over any other that could have been selected between the Red and Sabine rivers and within a reasonable distance of Natchitoches are those of health and good water. So long, therefore, as it may be deemed expedient to keep troops below the raft, a garrison may very properly [be] continued here.

Baton Rouge. When the situation of lower Louisiana with respect to her slave population is taken into consideration, the importance of this point as a military location will be more highly estimated, and truly the single circumstance of its being the only arsenal of arms in this region of country should of itself secure to it a garrison of several companies. New Orleans can protect itself; it has only to direct a proper organization of its effective force and all apprehension of danger must be at once removed, for its free citizens far outnumber the slave population. In this vicinity, however, the black population far outnumbers the white, but no apprehensions need be presumed upon this circumstance either here or at any other point on the lower Mississippi. Partial outrages, it is true, may be committed, but so long as the arsenal here is protected by a proper military force, there can not exist a just cause to apprehend anything like a concerted rising. Negroes no more than whites can effect much without arms and ammunition, and until they do procure them, be assured that be their feelings as hostile as they may, they will attempt nothing.

21

Having now considered the eligibility of the several locations along the lines designated, I will proceed in the next place to speak of the capabilities for defence of the posts themselves and of the fitness of their garrisons to secure us against all who might be disposed to disturb our quiet, leaving without remark the less important point in relation to health, comfort, and economy, as already as fully treated of in my previous reports as their consequence demands.

All the forts in the Indian country upon the lines which I have just traced out would seem to have been constructed solely with a view to the comfortable accommodation of the troops engaged in their erection and without even a thought about the strength of the garrisons that might eventually be assigned to them, or of the fact of their being important links in the great chain of connection between the northwest and southwest points of our interior frontier. To give proper garrisons suited to the very great superficial extent of the forts themselves, without taking into consideration the combustible materials of which they are built, would of itself exhaust the better part of our Infantry regiments, and that too without reserving a single disposable company to act as circumstances might require upon any part of our frontier.

But why need we furnish garrisons of such strength when surely no attack from the Indians or any other people can be apprehended? I answer that all our frontier posts should be viewed as though they were located in the immediate presence of a watchful enemy and should moreover be subjected to the same external police that might be considered as necessary in a time of war. Make our forts, as they should be, places of strength, small enough for complete defence by a single company of the present size and yet so constructed as to lodge upon an emergency several companies; and should it be thought necessary (as it should be) to station at any one of these particular posts a battalion or other force larger than a company, let it be cantoned in comfortable though temporary huts in the vicinity of the place, so as to derive protection from its guns. Within the enclosure of the fort all public property belonging to the post should be stored, so that at any moment the whole cantonment might be broken up without weakening the defences of the fort or endangering the safety of a single article of the public property; thus in fact to hold as a disposable force to act as circumstances might direct every company upon the frontiers with the exception of a single company as a garrison to each one of the forts.

The efficiency of this disposable force is not, however, to be determined by its numerical strength but by its adaptation to the particular service required of it, for while on the northwest frontier where the Indians are generally located upon the water courses, whence they derive their chief subsistence, and are found in passing to and fro to use the canoe almost exclusively, light armed foot would answer better than mounted men, so on the southwest frontier mounted men would answer better than any description of foot, for there canoes are seldom seen, the Indian is mounted on horseback on all occasions, and he is to be reached by those only who are mounted as well as he is. An Infantry man might as well be sent to chase the elk or deer as to pursue the Osage or Pawnee of the plains, as has unfortunately been more than once exemplified.

Seven years ago I earnestly recommended the employment of mounted men upon this frontier, being then, as I now am, convinced that we might with as much propriety look for ample protection to our foreign commerce from our seaboard fortresses without the aid of a naval force, as to expect that our interior commerce can be protected against the Tartars of the prairies by Infantry stationed at posts, without the assistance of a mounted force. Should the regiment of Dragoons (now being raised), when completely organized and in the field, fail to afford protection to the caravans passing through the country and at the same time to secure peace and quiet along the whole line from the Sabine to our northwestern boundary, I will admit that I am not only ignorant of the Indian character but greatly mistaken in the high estimate I had formed of the efficiency of mounted men.[9]

Fort Leavenworth, August 26, 1836

There is about as much propriety in calling this post *Fort* Leavenworth as there would be in calling an armed schooner a line of battle ship, for it is not only not a fort but is even devoid of the regularity of a common barrack. Of defences it has none. Colonel [Stephen Watts] Kearny, having very wisely recommended the erection of block houses, has under the authority of Brigadier General [Henry] Atkinson contracted for the building of two, or rather for the entire completion of one and the necessary timbers for the other, to be put up by his own men; both of them will be finished, it is believed, by December. . . . Should it be the intention of the government to keep up this post for any length of time, I would recommend that it have at all seasons some companies of Infantry in garrison. This I deem important if not indispensable, as without such provision this post and neighbourhood would be left without a guard whenever the Dragoons

[9] In 1833, by "An Act for the more perfect defence of the frontier," Congress established a regiment of Dragoons of ten companies, who were "liable to serve on horse, or foot, as the President may direct." In 1836 a second Dragoon regiment was authorized. *United States Statutes at Large,* IV, 652; V, 33.

should be called away upon any occasion of emergency or upon their customary summer campaign. Too much reliance ought not to be reposed upon the good faith and friendship of the tribes of Indians in this vicinity. We can not expect to keep a force sufficient to resist them effectually should they rise en masse, but we might at all events by some show of preparation and watchfulness prevent partial outbreaks.

Fort Mackinac, September, 1838

This place, which was without a garrison until a few days ago, has at present a company under the command of Captain [Gideon] Lowe of the 5th Infantry, who, being on his route from Fort Gratiot to Fort Winnebago, will proceed onwards so soon as the payment about being made to certain Indians shall have been completed. Of the company of Captain Lowe I have only to say that it is in as good condition as could reasonably be expected, when considered that it is composed mainly of recruits and that it has been of late almost constantly on the move. Its drill is certainly better than that of the company at Fort Howard, although of itself far from exact. Captain Lowe deserves credit for the pains which he has taken since his arrival to put the place in such order as not to call down the sneers of the Indians who might visit it.

Of the place itself and its armament I would remark that without a proper garrison they must alike suffer damage and destruction. I would that it met the intentions of the War Department to continue the occupancy of this post, which still holds a prominent place as it may relate to the consideration in which it is held by all the northwest Indians. It is still looked upon by them as Niagara was of old, by the Six Nations—as the *Stone House,* the chosen spot of the strongest of their white fathers and the proper residence of his children,

25

to whom as in duty bound they must attach themselves so long as by the flying of their flag they prove they rule the ascendant. There are here at this time more than 3,000 Indians, most of whom are aware that the present garrison will be removed so soon as the payment now about being made shall be completed and for the very reason that our army is so small as to render such a movement necessary. It is unfortunate that we should be compelled at this particular juncture to break up any of our frontier establishments, for there exists among all the Missouri, Mississippi, and lake Indians a feeling of distrust and dissatisfaction such as I have not before witnessed and which may grow into positive hostility unless they be checked by the assurance of watchfulness on the part of the military. It may be asked, whence this discontent among the Indians—the Indians' answer would be our treatment of them—as evidenced in our non-compliance with our treaty stipulations with many of them during the last two years. Let agents talk as they may, the Indians no longer entertain respect for our character as a people. If they act in obedience to our wishes, it is only because they stand in dread of our superior strength.

Fort Atkinson, September, 1840

You will doubtless have received ere this reaches you so full and satisfactory a description of this locality from those who selected it as a proper site for this establishment of a fort that it is needless I should say more than that it combines every requisite to a desirable residence (that of society excepted) and that the garrison stationed here will be found to exercise after a time such wholesome control of the Winnebagoes and their neighbours the Sioux, Sac, and Fox Indians, as to secure to us with the co-operation of the Dragoons of

Fort Leavenworth the quiet and peace of the whole Iowa country. Captain [Isaac] Lynde's company has not been paraded, and for the reason that, finding almost every man on fatigue, I have chosen to dispense with an inspection rather than call them from their several employments, knowing as I do that, work as they may, they will be scarcely able to finish the necessary buildings before the commencement of winter.

I spoke just now about the co-operation of the Dragoons of Fort Leavenworth as essential to the peace and quiet of this frontier, and I must now repeat that without such co-operation these desirable ends will be left at hazard, let the watchfulness and activity of the commandant here be as they may. Upon the headquarters of the Des Moines, not about here, do the Indians strike each other, and to that distance the influence of the Infantry garrison here can not reach. Scarcely a year passes without some serious affairs in that region of country, for being a fine hunting ground, it is visited at certain seasons by Missouri, Mississippi, and St. Peters Indians, who but seldom return to their respective homes without the loss or gain of some scalps. The occasional march of one or more companies of Dragoons to that quarter would serve to deter the several tribes from leaving their own immediate territories and thus that collision that can not take place without bloodshed.

Fort Wood, April 13, 1844

Forts Jackson, Pike, and Wood are essentially artillery posts, and yet they are garrisoned by Infantry. Deem me not intrusive if I inquire why this should be so, seeing that they are the most important posts in the United States, being upon its most exposed frontier. I say not that Infantry are unable

27

to garrison them properly but only that, as their armament consists exclusively of heavy guns, it should be entrusted to those who must be supposed to be well practised in the use of it. It may be urged that to give to these forts artillery garrisons would separate such commands to too great a distance from their regimental headquarters, but ought this to be considered? Should a proper distribution of this description of force be made to yield to meet the convenience of an unsuitable organization? I know not that I ever before expressed aloud the opinion I have all along entertained, that our artillery organization is a bad one and that instead of four regiments there should be but a single corps under the command of a colonel with as many captains and subalterns as might be judged necessary.

New Orleans Barracks, May 6, 1844

I was from the first opposed to the erection of these Barracks because I could never perceive a necessity for the stationing of troops either in or about New Orleans, and I challenge anyone to prove that such necessity does exist. When troops were stationed in the city before the sale of the fine old barracks, I very well recollect that the cry was, take the soldiers away, what do we want with them, we can protect ourselves, they are a nuisance. But when they were removed and the barracks sold, then all at once the want of soldiers was made clearly manifest. The purchased barracks were for rent and were actually rented for the accommodation of the very troops that had been ordered away in obedience to the earnest request of certain interested ones, and afterwards this want became even more apparent because much was to be gained by the heavy disbursements necessary in the purchase of land and the erection of permanent build-

Gold medal presented by Congress to Colonel George
Croghan in 1835.

FORT CRAWFORD
From a sketch by Seth Eastman, 1829.

FORT ARMSTRONG
From a sketch by Seth Eastman, 1848.

ings. Money, not the soldiers, was the object of these clamorous and interested ones. I beg that you look at a report of mine made about 15 years ago, and you will there find that then as now I was opposed to stationing troops here and for reasons which appeared to me conclusive at the time.[10] But without especial reference to that report I would now ask, why keep a garrison here, from whom do we apprehend danger—from a transatlantic power, then garrison the forts near the balize, the lake, and the bayou; from the Negroes, then strongly garrison Baton Rouge to prevent their seizing upon the arms, for without them they will attempt nothing. New Orleans needs none of our soldiers, for besides her finely disciplined and trained volunteer corps she has in her quadroon population the best possible description of force in the event of a Negro insurrection, for bold, daring, and active, and thoroughly acquainted with the character of the blacks, they would outdo the whites even in their utmost efforts, for besides that they themselves are slave holders, they are also aware that unless an insurrection should be put down immediately, they as colored people would be identified with the blacks and would perish with them upon the coming down of troops from the country above to the assistance of the whites.

Fort Jesup, May 14, 1844

I was once, say in 1827, opposed to the continuance of a garrison at this post, but since that time our outward relations have so materially altered as to cause a corresponding change in the opinion which I entertained at that early period.[11] Texas has virtually established her independence, and thus has arisen the necessity on our part for watchfulness upon

[10] See remarks of Croghan in his report of 1829, pages 11–12.
[11] See the report of 1827, page 10.

this frontier. So long as the territory was under Mexican rule we had nothing to apprehend; a wilderness lay between us, and there was neither opportunity nor inducement to keep up any intercourse in the least calculated to imbroil us, but now the case is altered. The way is open and the communication direct and daily. Texas is too much of our own blood for a neighbouring independent sovereignty; claims will be advanced, indulgences and privileges expected, and many things done upon the strength of this tie of kindred, calculated to test our forbearance. What induced President Houston to grant a piratical commission to Colonel Snively, but the belief that no cognizance would be taken of the most atrocious acts of hostility committed upon the Mexicans by the Colonel and his myrmidons even within our acknowledged limits?[12] At this moment we are more likely to be imbroiled with our frontier Indians through the acts of Texas than from any other cause, for her course of policy and action as it respects the Indians is so eccentric that difficulties will arise between them and thus imbroil us in spite of ourselves, for the Indians one and all look upon us as responsible for every act of Texas.

But apart from all view of Texas, the location of a respectable force at this point will be found to oppose a strong

[12] Jacob S. Snively, a colonel in the Texas Army, was granted permission in 1843 to raise a force and proceed to the Texas frontier along the Red River to capture a rich Mexican train which had left Independence, Missouri, for Santa Fé. Snively failed in his purpose and his party was captured and disarmed by United States troops under Captain Philip St. George Cooke who were protecting the train while it remained in United States territory. After long controversy it was decided that the Texans had been on Texas soil when forced to disarm, and the United States paid for the captured arms. See footnotes in *The Writings of Sam Houston, 1813–1863,* edited by Amelia W. Williams and Eugene C. Barker, II, 39, 451, and the references listed there. A well-balanced account of the Snively affair appears in Otis E. Young, *The West of Philip St. George Cooke, 1809–1895* (Glendale, 1955), 109–35.

counteracting influence to the efforts that the foreign and domestic abolitionists may make and perhaps are making among the slaves below on the Red and Mississippi rivers, for the blacks are not so blind as to be unable to see that, however great might be their accession of force in their downward march, they would be most certainly pursued, overtaken, and cut to pieces by the troops from Fort Jesup before they could reach Baton Rouge, where along they could arm themselves.

Fort Towson, June 4, 1844
This fort is upon the site of the old post abandoned in 1827. You are aware that it is inland and six miles from the nearest point of the Red River. Such a location would be highly objectionable upon the upper Mississippi or any of its tributaries north of the Missouri River, where all Indian communication is by water, but such is not the case in the region of country lying upon the Red and Arkansas rivers or their tributaries, where the travel is altogether by land, a canoe being but seldom seen.

The cost of provisioning an inland post must be greater than would attend upon one situated on a navigable stream, but then the better health would more than compensate for that additional expence, besides which, by acting without reference to the convenience of navigation, such locations might be selected as would be best calculated to gain the end in view, a perfect control of the Indian movements.

Fort Smith, June 27, 1844
On the bank of the Arkansas River within a mile of this place a work to be called Fort Smith has been commenced and which has already cost, I am told, more than *$100,000.*

31

It scarcely comes within my province to speak of this work, well aware that it is exclusively a *civil* undertaking, but as it seems that soldiers are to be called to complete it, I must be permitted to remark that, however willing I might be to have them labour upon works of real utility and importance, I am not at all disposed to order them to waste their time and strength upon such as can never be of any public benefit and which are required only at the call of some political aspirant merely to advance his own private ends. The work may be said to be but just commenced; at all events it has not progressed very far. If then we consider the time and money that must be spent before it can be completed (a consummation I devoutly wish may never be realized), would it not be better to give to Arkansas at once *$200,000* than to expend the amount in the completion of a work that will stand as a lasting monument to the folly of the administration under whose rule it was commenced, for it will not be known after a little time that it was granted to the earnest and oft repeated declarations and prayers of Arkansas. No troops are wanted in this section of country. I advise then that the companies under Major [William] Hoffman be withdrawn and placed at some point where they may at least *seem* to be of use, so soon as their present quarters become uninhabitable, which must be at no distant date.

If Congress chooses to appropriate money for the completion of the work, why be it so. That makes it not at all incumbent on you to give it a garrison, and garrison it I would not. Congress can not constitutionally interfere in the distribution of our military force, although it may squander millions upon any project however wild and visionary. Some of the Arkansas great men, in boasting of their agency in obtaining appropriations for this work, speak of it as a place of refuge to which to fly in the event of a sudden outbreak of the Indians. A most original idea, truly, that to escape from an enemy you must flee towards him, not from him, as would be the case in every attempt to reach this *place of refuge,* it being directly on the line of the Indian territory.

But I have already said perhaps more than enough about this folly of follies, and will close. . . .

2: THE FORTS

CROGHAN did not limit himself to a discussion of the proper location of forts in the light of frontier military needs. He was concerned as well with the minutiae of garrison defense, and he did not lack material on which to vent his indignation. Remarks on fortifications and on the sorry state of quarters in general occupy large sections of the inspection reports.

It might seem that Croghan was too harsh in his judgments, that his perfectionism led him to criticize too severely the posts he visited. It was his business, of course, to point out deficiencies to be corrected rather than any excellences he might discover, but other visitors to the western posts corroborate the Inspector General's black picture. At any rate, the reports of Croghan should dispel any romantic conception of the frontier fortresses as tight little castles, always in a state of perfect police and repair. It took a constant struggle just to keep the places livable.

STATE OF FORTIFICATIONS

The western forts were set up in the wilderness as citadels of American power and authority, to serve not only as actual fortresses of defense but also as symbols of strength by which to overawe the Indians. In both of these elements Croghan found the forts wanting. He praises whatever he can, but the general picture he presents is of widespread unpreparedness. And he particularizes his criticisms. The size or type of construction is unsuitable, the defenses are in a rundown condition, or there are inadequacies in ordnance. Croghan was often unhappy with what he found, and he offers explicit or implied suggestions to remedy the defects.

Fort Brady, July 9, 1826

Why this place is dignified with the name of fort I can not imagine, for it is fitted for neither offensive or defensive purposes. So badly is it designed for either that in the event of an attack the danger of the troops composing its garrison would be lessened only when they had gained the open spot without the line of pickets. The two block houses placed on diagonal corners of the place, which is in the form of a parallelogram, are in themselves built of good and stout materials and might with some alteration of their embrasures, loop holes, and roofs be made quite defensible, but they would be strong only when disconnected from the great extent of combustible materials which they have now to flank. If my eye deceives me not, the circumference of the place can not fall short of 2,400 feet, an extent, it may be said, not too great to be defended by its present force, 140 effectives, against any desultory attack, particularly of Indians. To this I agree, provided no part of the lines to be flanked be made of combustible materials; and further, that the attack be made at the hour I might select. If these be not granted, I disagree, and moreover assert that in the present condition of the defences it is in the power of any dozen men who might choose to watch an opportunity to set fire to the place and cause the garrison to seek safety by flight to the open space without the line of pickets.

Apart, too, from these objections, the work itself is endangered by the position of the stables and barns, which are placed on the bank of the river so near to one of the block houses that to fire them would be to jeopard the whole establishment. In objecting to the title given to this place, I must in candor allow that the necessary precautions seem not to be taken to guard against accidents, for of the sentinels posted, but one, he on the water side, can see over the pickets or is of the least use. The rest walk on the ground within the work where their heads can not only not appear above the pickets, but even reach to the height of the loop holes. Lieutenant Colonel [William] Lawrence promises to remedy this by erecting platforms for the sentinels and raising banquettes along the pickets, so as in the event of accident to have the loop holes of some service.

Fort Howard, July 27, 1826

Neither officer nor soldier feels that he is within the walls of a fort unless he see it completely garnished and prepared for immediate action, as this work and every other on the frontier should be; but this is not, neither is Fort Brady or Mackinac. My fears are therefore that those which I am yet to visit are too nearly in the same condition. It is not that an Indian attack may be expected here or against any other of our military posts that I wish to see this and others on the frontier in complete equipment, but (apart from the feelings it would engender in the garrison themselves) . . . because I wish to produce an effect upon the Indians and thus put a stop to those murders which are too frequently committed by them. Were one tribe to say to another (and there is great intercourse among all of them), "The soldiers of the great Father in our country are warriors, they never sleep, they are constantly on the watch for the enemy"—such exaggerated notions of the prowess of our military would soon become current among them, that not even in thought would an Indian commit a violence upon a white man, however remote from the settlements or a military force.

But if my information be not incorrect (and my personal observations tell me that it is not), these exaggerated notions of our strength have not been created and are far from existing. Our military have lost character among them, for they have found no warriors, according to their estimates of worth, but common people, who build forts and carry about with them arms through fear of being driven out of the country and who, under charge of overseers, do under compulsion all sorts of menial labour degrading to a true warrior. The fact of the expulsion of the British trader from our territory tends more towards the protection of our frontier than all the show of military strength which we make along it. It speaks home to the Indians, telling them that their British Father, no longer strong, is compelled to yield his lands to the American Father and that they must therefore be careful how they affect the Americans, as in the event of their getting into difficulty they must rely upon themselves, as no help can any longer be afforded them.

To return to the subject from which I have so long wandered, the ordnance. With a view to test the state of preparation of the garrison for defence, in whatever this particular arm is concerned, I directed a few shells to be fired. The officer of ordnance begged time to prepare some fuses, as they required paring down, being all too large for his shells. Some hours were occupied in this preparation; at length the fuses were driven and a trial made, sufficient to prove that but few present knew either how to prepare a shell, to load the piece, or to fire it when loaded, and that the fuses which cost such length of time to get ready were not equitable, nor to be made so by any means at hand to use. Out of perhaps a dozen shells fired, not more than two burst. In nothing that I have said do I intend a reflection upon the ordnance officer, Lieutenant [William B.] Thompson, who is an active and intelligent young gentleman.

Fort Snelling, May, 1827

I know not by whom the lines of this fort were first traced, nor can I state at what expenditure of public funds the work has been thus far advanced, but of these facts I am confident, that it might have been contracted for at a much less cost, that it covers an extent of ground too large by three fourths for any garrison that can be permanently given it, and that it has deprived Colonel Snelling of the satisfaction of having a command that might fairly compare in degree of instruction with any other in service.

Fort Howard, June, 1828

This fort bears as nearly as may be a resemblance to those military stations which some years back were built by the frontier inhabitants of the western states as rallying points in the event of Indian disturbances. Whatever about them was found necessary for the convenience of a large congregation of families for a length of time is to be seen here. Stables, hen houses, cow houses, *private* work shops, root houses, wash houses in any number and without any order. The very lines of defence themselves are made to sustain a part in the preservation of the resemblance by furnishing points of egress to the various conveniences just enumerated. The number of gates, public and private, may be rated at fifteen.

It is expected that Major [David E.] Twiggs, on assuming command, will very soon view all this as he ought and restore the place to something like a becoming appearance. I would not have believed that these nuisances are of a date subsequent to my visit in 1826. They existed then, but under whose command they grew up I know not. He who would have peace himself and who desires to bequeath it to his successor in command should have nothing about him claiming *individual* ownership. Give but leave to erect a stable, and even although it afterwards prove a nuisance, an order to pull it down would be viewed as an act of military oppression and as bearing grievously hard upon the person who out of his own private purse paid for its erection.

Fort Crawford, September, 1840

In my report of August, 1838, I stated that a house was being built for the commanding officer upon the site of the one formerly occupied by him, that is to say by the commandant of the post, at the same time expressing my regret that authority had been granted for the expenditure of a large amount of money so unnecessarily, as there were already more than government allowance of good quarters within the fort.[1] I must now report that the house with its out buildings is very nearly completed, at what cost I know not—that pickets of hewn timber and 16 or 18 feet high have been put around the yards of the officers' quarters on the east and west faces of the square and joined to the men's barracks in such a way as to form with them a complete inclosure; and that there are now being erected block houses of hewn stone at diagonal corners of the square. The pickets serve to keep the men within the fort, as was contemplated I suppose in their erection, but what purpose within the reach of possibilities

[1] See the report of 1838, page 46.

the block houses are to serve I am at a loss to conjecture. It is not at this post alone that large and unnecessary disbursements of money have been allowed. Fort Howard, Fort Armstrong, and Jefferson Barracks have had in like manner their full share.

Fort Atkinson, July 27, 1842

Twenty-eight thousand dollars and more have already been expended upon this post, nearly fourteen thousand beyond the amount appropriated by Congress, and five thousand dollars more are wanted to complete the work. More than thirty thousand dollars expended, when one thousand would have answered every necessary end. Ought this to have been? Fort Atkinson of the Missouri with all its ample accommodations for an entire regiment did not cost a fourth nor did Fort Madison of the Mississippi a sixtieth part of thirty thousand dollars; and yet they were thought good enough, and even in Indian times, strong enough. No temporary work, such as this ought to be, should cost more than five hundred dollars or require a longer time than a month in its erection, and such would have been the case but a few years ago when no one ever thought of calling upon the quartermaster for more than glass and nails. It is mortifying to know that upon this place and Fort Crawford more than fifty thousand dollars have been unnecessarily expended within the last five years.

Fort Mackinac, October 7, 1843

Captain [Martin] Scott is entitled to great credit for his untiring efforts to repair and improve the appearance of his post, which is now in point of order and extreme neatness perhaps without a parallel in the country. But he has not confined his attention exclusively to his parade and quarters. He has built up the dilapidated walls of the fort, put up palisades where they were wanted, has made a fine walk protected on the upper side by a stone wall along the steep hillside and reaching to the front gate, in a word, has repaired or renewed everything very substantially and with taste, and all with an expense of $7.50 only to the government. But has not all this, it may be asked, been accomplished at the expense of the drill? I answer—his command is better instructed than it was in June, 1842, and further that the clothing, arms, and equipments of his men are in the finest condition and in every way serviceable.

Fort Gibson, July 1, 1844

Congress has appropriated, I am informed, $30,000 for the erection of barracks at this place. This being the case, it is hoped that a site will be immediately fixed upon and the buildings commenced after so[me] well-matured plan not to be deviated from, as we would avoid the confusion and want of order which seem to prevail in the arrangement of the various buildings which are scattered about Fort Gibson. I know not how many acres are covered by the fort proper, the Dragoon barracks, and the many other buildings scattered about amidst weeds, gardens, patches of corn, old hay stacks, etc., but be they few or many, a daily detail of 200 men would be required to keep them in a proper degree of cleanliness.

So soon as the new barracks with all the stables, necessary store houses, etc., are completed, demolish the old fort, together with the out buildings, corn fields, etc., which now disfigure the plain, and as much health may be expected as can be found upon any fresh water river in this latitude.

Fort Des Moines, July 25, 1845

The square space comprised within the lines marked out by the various buildings appertaining to the post can not fall short of 40 acres. An entire regiment could not attend properly to the police of so large a surface even under the most favorable circumstances. What then can be expected of two skeleton companies?

CONDITION OF QUARTERS

One fact seems to emerge before all others in Croghan's account of the barracks and quarters: they were always in need of repair. The frequent poor planning, the hasty construction, the reliance on temporary structures which stretched out beyond their reasonable length of service, and the use of soldier labor all contributed to this state of affairs. Indeed, one can hardly speak of the building of the forts as though it were a one-time process. The fact is that the forts were in an almost constant state of rebuilding, and every report of Croghan echoes with demands for stop-gap repairs or for extensive replacement. Only occasionally does the Inspector General arrive at a time when repairs have all been accomplished and everything is in a state of perfection.

Croghan was always alert for the well-being of the men. Plenty of ventilation was one of his panaceas, and he probably had a point, considering the crowded barracks where the men slept in bunks built for four and sometimes for six!

These bunks and their attached arms racks were inspected regularly by Croghan and formed the matter for a separate section in each of his reports. Regulations in regard to their construction did not result in uniformity—except that in general they seem to have suffered from a rickety condition. "Crazy things indeed," as Croghan noted. And the reason was not hard to find, for it grew out of the two mutually incompatible requirements. The bunks had to be strongly made and sturdy enough to support the assigned occupants. But on the other hand, they had to be easily taken apart to rid them of the bed bugs which abounded in all the garrisons. Croghan found few places which had resolved the difficulty.

Fort Howard, June, 1828

The present allowance of transportation in *kind* is far too small for a time of peace and might be increased without inconvenience, but until a change is authorized, enforce the existing regulation if you would have it bear equally throughout. What is an officer to do with his furniture which, although of some amount, is but sufficient for his family and will be wanted at the post to which he is ordered? Sell it if he can; at all events leave it behind (unless he can get private transportation) and supply himself anew on his arrival at his post. He can do not better under the regulation. The quarters at none of our posts are furnished as they should be, and hence all this difficulty and frequent want of comfort. No officer would encumber himself with a parcel of tables, bedsteads, sideboards, etc., were he informed that all these things were already in place for him at the post to which he is about to depart, and this necessary furniture could be made at a comparatively trifling cost to the government, as the work could be done by the mechanics of the army, who even now are employed on such service but for private uses.

Fort Leavenworth, March 31, 1829

The same mistake has been committed here that I have elsewhere more than once complained of—too much has been undertaken, everything is upon too vast a scale to warrant a belief in its completion agreeably to the original plan of the

43

projector (at least within any reasonable time). A great deal has been done, much more in truth than could have been expected of a garrison so reduced by sickness; still the work is not half accomplished, either as to labour or disbursements of money. A good hospital has been erected, and four houses, originally intended to quarter one company each (though now occupied by officers), have been put up and very nearly completed, but there yet remains to be provided for officers' quarters, store houses, guard house, magazine, etc., etc.

Baton Rouge, May 9, 1829

The barracks here are in an unfinished state and have so remained for years, why, I am unable [to] explain. I would that they could be finished forthwith, because they are suffering greatly by exposure to the weather, and finished in such a way as to render them as far as practicable convenient and comfortable, even although the original plan of the buildings be deviated from. Galleries are wanted on the rear of the lines of barracks of similar construction to those on the front, and they will be ordered too, I am sure, when it is considered that in this climate the want of roomy and comfortable quarters is sure to be attended by want of health.

Fort Wood, May 25, 1829

The form of the bunks is not perhaps in conformity with that prescribed by regulation, and is certainly not suited to this locality and climate, which would cause us to separate rather than crowd sleepers together. The widest bunks that I have seen hitherto are less than three feet wide, but these are at least five feet and of three tiers in height, and each tier calculated to lodge three instead of two persons, as usual.

FORT HOWARD
From *Vues et Souvenirs de l'Amérique du Nord,*
by Francis de Castelnau (Paris, 1842).

FORT SNELLING
From *The United States Illustrated in Views of City and
Country,* by Charles A. Dana (New York, 1854).

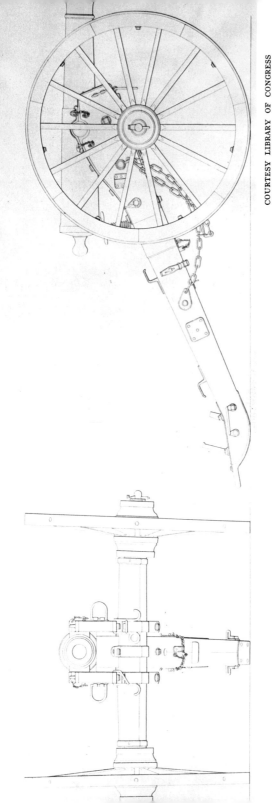

6-PDR. GUN AND CARRIAGE.

SIX-POUNDER GUN
From *Artillery for the Land Service,*
by Alfred Mordecai (1841).

Fort Howard, June 28, 1831

State of quarters. Those for both officers and men alike almost in a state of ruin. The commanding officer's quarters and the building at the end of the southeast range alone excepted, and they will doubtless be used in the arrangement of the new quarters now about to be erected.

Bunks and arm racks. Neither were ever in conformity with regulation, and they are now after 8 or 10 years' service (as may be supposed) crazy things indeed.

Fort Leavenworth, August 26, 1836

The stables are execrable, worse than the worst stables at the worst country taverns that I have yet seen, added to which their location is bad, being so distant from the barracks and guard house as to be completely out of the range of proper protection.

Fort Snelling, August 16, 1838

The large store house, used by the subsistence and quartermaster department, leaks badly and ought to be reshingled. The stables require new roofing. The magazine shed is falling down. In a word, every building within the work, with the exception of the northwest block house, leaks badly, some more—others less. As this post will be continued in all probability for twelve or fifteen years longer, I would suggest the propriety of ordering a board of examination into the state and condition of the buildings above stated, with a view to determine what should be done in relation to them. The range of officers' quarters is of wood and is much out of repair— its entire gallery requires renewal, which will not be wondered at when it is considered that it has been in use nineteen or twenty years.

Fort Crawford, August 20, 1838

A house for the commanding officer is now being built upon the site of the one formerly occupied by him but recently pulled down as no longer tenantable. This I regard as an unnecessary expenditure of the public money, as there are abundance of quarters within the fort itself to furnish even more than the regulation allowance to all the officers that may henceforth be stationed here. The quarters too are better than can be found at almost any other post in the country.

Fort Winnebago, August 25, 1838

Bunks in bad condition and irreparable. The very circumstance which induced their being built as they are, with timber far beyond the usual size, has contributed to their present craziness, for although size may give strength, it at the same time affords, as in this instance, greater surface for the growth of this pest of the country—the *bed bugs*, which by compelling an almost constant overhauling of both bunk and furniture necessarily hastens the destruction of both.

Fort Brady, September 12, 1838

The bunks are defective in this, that the lower tier, being on the floor itself, must of course remain damp for some time after the chambers have been washed out. I would remark also that the chambers themselves from want of proper ventilation have in damp and warm weather a foul, unpleasant smell, which must become worse as the timbers of which the buildings are erected decay. To obviate this (in some degree at least), windows must be made on the rear of the several apartments to correspond with those on the front. . . .

Should a garrison be continued here for any length of time, everything must be made anew. The quarters and other buildings have stood their day and are now not worth any further repairs. The block houses are still sound and would be worth removing, which must be done provided a new fort is to be built, as the present one is too large by one half for even a garrison of two companies on the present establishment. But apart from the too great extent of the fort as a reason for a change in the position of the block houses is another which of itself would make it necessary. The river has risen so high as to reach far within the line of pickets, to the endangering of them as well as the block house which flanks the water front.

Fort Gratiot, June 21, 1842

I would advise that the pickets which enclose this place (those on the south face alone excepted) be pulled down, as they are even worse than useless. Besides that they present no wall of defence, they completely shut out the healthful and refreshing lake winds, which now percolating through their decayed and rotting crevices reach the garrison in the guise of offensive miasm. The pickets being removed, enlarge the area of the place by one half at least. Surround the whole by a substantial paling 8 feet high, and health and comfort and appearance all will be promoted without the sacrifice of a single advantage in any sense of the term.

Fort Brady, June 25, 1842

The quarters of both officers and men are in a dilapidated condition. The floors of all of them have sunk more or less. The doors no longer swing perpendicularly on their hinges; the porticoes are rotten; in truth, nothing is as it should be save the roofing, which is sound and tight throughout.

Fort Crawford, July 11, 1842

No complaints on the score of quarters can be made, and

47

satisfaction even among the younger officers, always the first to complain, is expressed throughout. Carpenters are at work under the direction of the acting assistant quartermaster of the post in renewing certain timbers of the porches, repairing steps, etc., but the cost of the whole will be but trifling, and the work will be completed before the end of the month.

Bunks and arm racks. Both were so well made and of such durable materials under the searching eye of Brigadier General [Zachary] Taylor when the barracks were being built that they are very nearly as good and serviceable as they were in the first instance, when I reported them to be in exact conformity with regulation. Complaints are made of their bulkiness and the difficulty of taking them apart as often as could be wished to rid them of the bugs which are frequently very troublesome, but this inconvenience must remain and without remedy so long as we have wooden bunks, for they can not be made more portable and answer at the same time for the accommodation of four men each.

Fort Winnebago, July 5, 1842

None of the quarters are in good repair, though such of them as are occupied are sufficiently so to render [them] comfortable. It is perhaps not unknown to you that all the quarters have cellar or basement rooms, and thus it is that the cost for repairs has been greater than it would have been had the buildings been entirely above ground, for it has been found to be impossible to keep the lower rooms dry, and of course the floors, etc., soon decay and rot. Even with porticoes, such as are before the men's quarters, this has not been prevented, and where there are none, as is the case with the officers' quarters, the rain will obtrude, and in the winter the snow is not unfrequently several feet deep on the steps and

48

for the time completely cutting off all communication with the lower apartments from without. I do not recommend an appropriation for the repair of any of the quarters unless it be the intention of the Department to send more troops to add to the present garrison. All that need be asked is a small sum (say $100) to be placed in the hands of the commanding officer for the repair of the steps and doorways leading into some of the quarters. If, however, more troops be sent up, extensive repairs will be requisite; in truth the whole of the northern range of quarters is in a very dilapidated condition.

Fort Snelling, September 3, 1843

All the officers' quarters, the surgeon's excepted, have been painted since I was last here, and thus far something towards bettering their appearance has been effected but nothing to render them more comfortable has been even commenced, which is to be regretted as some of them leak so badly (besides being in other respects out of repair) that whenever it rains, buckets, pans, etc., are put in requisition to catch the water that would otherwise deluge the furniture.

Fort Atkinson, September 7, 1843

A requisition for 19 stoves for the hospital and officers' and men's quarters has been forwarded to the quartermaster at St. Louis, which I trust may be immediately met, so that they may be here before the commencement of the winter. Many of the chimneys smoke so badly that no comfort can be expected without stoves, and more than this, a great saving of fuel will be made, for to supply the *fire places* the daily labor of 25 axe men and five teamsters is requisite during the winter, whereas 10 axe men and 2 teamsters can supply the stoves.

Fort Brady, September 29, 1843

The appearance of the post has greatly improved within the last 16 months; new floors have been laid in most of the quarters, the porches have undergone material though perhaps not sufficient repairs, some of the picketing has been renewed; in a word, Captain [Alexander] Johnston, by turning everything to the best account, has made the old fort look quite well again. Let not this last remark, however, induce you the less strongly to advocate the propriety of an appropriation for the erection of a new work, if the purpose be to continue a garrison at Sault Ste Marie for any length of time, for truly patch as you may, the old barrack will fall to pieces from its own rottenness in a few years.

Madison Barracks, November 1, 1843

The quarters are in good repair, and as I had a right to expect, they are clean and neat. It is but seldom indeed that neglect of proper police can be justly charged against any of our garrisons. The drill may be sometimes neglected, but police, I might almost say, never.

The bunks are all old and not of the same pattern throughout; some have the rack or stand attached, others are without them, the arms being placed in a rack made apart and fastened to the wall. Though old and a little crazy, they may be made to answer for some years to come. The chief objection to an old bunk is that when once infected by bugs, it can not be rid of them without great inconvenience and trouble, for if it be taken down with a view to a thorough examination, the chances are that it can not be put together again.

New Orleans Barracks, May 6, 1844

The quarters of both officers and men are in good repair

50

and kept in the neatest possible order. I can not say anything, however, in favor of the plan of the soldiers' quarters or rather of their arrangement. The houses separately considered are well enough, yet placed as they are around a small square, they so completely interrupt all free circulation of the air and reflect upon each other the scorching mid-day sun that the heat is often times overpowering.

Fort Towson, June 4, 1844

There are but few bunks at the post, and such as there are are worth nothing. The men, to avoid the bed bugs, which are in countless numbers, sleep either upon the galleries or the floor of their quarters. Captain [Charles O.] Collins will in the course of the summer furnish all the quarters with new bunks, so constructed as to be easily taken down, an essential quality where they require to be so frequently overhauled. The arms racks are but little better than the bunks and improperly made as well as badly arranged. They too will be attended to by the assistant quartermaster in due season.

Fort Washita, June 19, 1844

All the officers, whether of the staff or line, with the exception of Colonel [William S.] Harney and the senior medical officer, Major [Benjamin L.] Beall, and the adjutant, live in temporary huts of round logs, placed without regard to order. These gentlemen occupy the only two sets of quarters that are called permanent, and they are so designated, not that they are built of durable materials, but because some pains have been taken in the manner of their erection and that they are larger than the other buildings, being of one story with four rooms, besides a hall and front porch, each of ten feet in width. The quarters of the men are con-

51

venient and comfortable; each company has two blocks or sets of houses, containing two rooms of 17 by 19 feet, separated by a hall or passage nine or ten feet wide. These houses are of oak logs hewn on the inside, and though built with no eye to permanency, they will nevertheless answer every purpose for some years or until the command can make bricks and provide the necessary lumber for the erection of barracks of a better and more durable description. The frame of a very large house for officers' quarters has been erected, and every effort will be made to finish the building by the close of autumn, but the difficulty of procuring lumber is so great that no calculation as to time can be relied on. Plank is sometimes brought up the Washita River, but has never been sold under $40, and such as the men have sawed has been from logs hauled fifteen or more miles, there being no timber hereabouts suited to such a purpose.

Fort Smith, June 27, 1844

The quarters of the commandant alone are in good condition. All the others, whether of officer or soldier, are rapidly approaching to dilapidation, and although at present habitable, they will in the course of a year or two tumble down. In truth, but for the pains taken to avert such calamity by the use of props and other modes of strengthening, some of them would have been down ere this. They all stand upon wooden posts two or three feet high, which rotting of course cause the superstructure to settle and in some cases to separate, as none of them are held together by girders as is the case with the house of the commandant. All the buildings are of wood put together somewhat after the Canadian manner, short logs let into grooved uprights and with no seeming regard to strength or durability.

Fort Gibson, July 1, 1844

Frequent complaints of the condition of these quarters (within the fort) have doubtless reached you. I need therefore say but little more than that they are sadly out of repair and besides are very uncomfortable, though by no means so much so as they were a short time ago before the pickets were pulled down and windows cut in the back of the men's quarters. Pent up as they were before this change was made, the wonder is not that the men became sick but that any lived. The range of the thermometer during the summer months has always been much higher within the fort than at the hospital, where there is a free circulation of air. I am persuaded that in suffering the pickets to remain and in neglecting to furnish proper ventilation to the men's quarters by cutting windows, more deaths have been caused than can be justly charged to Indian rifles during the whole of the Florida war.

Fort Des Moines, July 25, 1845

The officers' and men's quarters, hospital, store rooms, etc., are built of round unbarked logs cut in the adjacent forest and finished in the plainest manner. Some expence might have been saved had common clapboards and weight poles been used for the roofs instead of shingles with nails and puncheons or thick slabs of oak for the floors in place of plank, but I state not this by way of complaint against the captain, whom I would sooner compliment, although I still insist, as I did when speaking some years ago of the useless and extravagant expenditure of money at Fort Atkinson, that no frontier post established for a temporary purpose or for occupancy not to exceed six or seven years ought to cost more than five hundred dollars.

Fort Snelling, August 6, 1845

Some work has been done upon the hospital, and 60 men are now busily employed upon the men's barracks. The stone barrack range is undergoing a thorough repair, which may be completed by the close of the present month, and the wooden range, which has been pulled down, will be replaced by a stone one of equal size though better arranged before the 1st of November. The season is now too far advanced to commence upon the officers' quarters this year, but building materials are being collected so as to insure their completion before the close of the autumn of 1846. It is not, I understand, the intention of the Department to repair the present quarters but to erect new ones. Whether they will be built within or without the fort has not as yet [been] determined. Captain [Samuel M.] Plummer, who will have charge of the work, decides in favor of the outside on the score of economy irrespective of other considerations, perhaps insisting that the removal of the old buildings and the erection of new ones upon their foundations would cost, owing to the confined space in which the work must be carried on, much more than similar buildings on the open space without the fort, but his action in the matter will be regulated by the authorities in Washington. The companies are in tents, well arranged immediately west and within 100 paces of the fort, where they will remain until their quarters are finished. The police of the encampment, that is to say, all the daily garrison details and duties, seem to be conducted with regularity, and every one is pleased with his temporary residence, which as yet has not, nor is it expected that it will, exercise unfavorable influence upon the health of the command.

3: ADMINISTRATION
AND SERVICES

THE FOOD, clothing, medical care, and pay of the soldiers garrisoned at the western forts all came under the scrutiny of the Inspector General. The inspection of everyday details which was required by regulations was scrupulously carried out by Croghan. He took pains to see that the soldiers were adequately provided with the pay and supplies which the *General Regulations* authorized. In these mundane affairs the Inspector General no doubt helped as much to maintain a smoothly running army as in the more dramatic elements of frontier fortification or military discipline and instruction.

ADMINISTRATION

One section of the reports was invariably headed "Administration," a term that had a strict and technical meaning in the *General Regulations*. Under this head the Inspector General investigated "the just direction and economical application or expenditure of the several sums of money appropriated by Congress for the army, or military defence of the country on land." More particularly, the term was restricted to mean the "interior administration of corps." Here the points to be inspected were clearly detailed: "It particularly regards the regularity of payments made to the troops; regularity in issues or supplies of subsistence, clothing, and all other allowances accorded to the troops; and finally, the quality of those articles."[1]

[1] Paragraph 299, Article 37, *General Regulations for the Army*, 1825.

Important as was this section of army life, Croghan generally dismissed it in his reports with only a brief statement, and these statements were almost identical from year to year and post to post. The reason was that he found little to criticize on this score. Everywhere he went, Croghan heard few complaints about unfairness or delays in according to each soldier the pay, rations, and clothing to which he was entitled. The following brief extracts from the annual reports indicate this general satisfaction.

Fort Howard, August 31, 1828
Every allowance to which the soldier is by law entitled is most studiously furnished him.

Fort Brady, July 20, 1834
Pay, rations, and clothing continue to be received as contemplated by the framers of the book of regulations. Our soldiers surely have no cause for dissatisfaction, the allowances accorded to them by law and the regulations are more liberal than those granted to the soldiers of any other power on earth, and more than all, those allowances are never improperly withheld.

Fort Winnebago, August 7, 1834
Here as at all other posts there is a scrupulous exactness in issuing to the soldier all the allowances granted by law and regulation. It has sometimes, though rarely, occurred here as elsewhere that pay or clothing was not received at the expected time, but such delays have in every instance been attributable to untoward circumstances, never to neglect.

Fort Leavenworth, 1838
Administration—Correct, unless in this . . . that many of

the command have not yet received the entire amount of clothing to which they are entitled.

Fort Snelling, August 16, 1838
Administration. No complaints have or can with propriety be made on this score. Everything allowed by law to the soldier has been as regularly rendered to him as circumstances have permitted.

Fort Atkinson, September 7, 1843
The government allowance of pay, clothing, and subsistence is liberal, usually of the best quality, and never withheld unless by sentence of a court martial.

CLOTHING
Although Croghan found that the *Regulations* were well adhered to in the issuing of clothing to the soldiers, he was not so well pleased with the type and quality of the clothes thus issued. Again and again he complained about the injustice involved in making no distinctions for kind of service in the allowance of clothing. His heart goes out to the men in the West, whose heavy fatigue duty in the building of roads and the clearing of land took heavy toll of their regular issue and whose only recourse was to draw extra clothing at their own expense. He was interested in the design of the clothing and its suitability to the kind of service, and he did not overlook the importance of a proper fit. All this no doubt was part of his inherent military spirit, for what could be more unmilitary than a parade spoiled by poorly designed and ill-fitting uniforms!

Individual clothing, then as now, was an obvious item to be inspected by the Inspector General when he made his rounds. Croghan's reports give ample evidence that he did not by-pass this opportunity to check on the neatness and care of the private soldier.

57

Fort Mackinac, July 14, 1826

Clothing [is] good of its kind and received to the amount authorized by the law, but neither in character nor amount suited to the wants of the soldier on a cold exposed frontier like this, especially when he is during the summer cutting in the midst [of] mosquitoes his fire wood for the winter—digging canals—making roads—preparing materials for the erection of houses which neither he nor his officer is to live in—collecting hay where it is frequently waist deep in the water—following the tail of a plough—or at the spade in the gardens, and in the winter harnessed to sleds like a horse, to drag into his garrison through snow two feet deep, the wood, forage, or whatever else he may have collected during the summer. Two pairs of boots and two pairs of shoes per year serve a soldier at Fort Mifflin[2] or even in the harbour of New York, but they must be made of better leather than I have yet seen if they last him here. The service upon the Atlantic board is that of parade—here of constant fatigue and exposure. Let the disbursement then be proportioned to the service performed and the actual wants of the case.

Fort Jesup, May 3, 1829

Clothing. Not well marked in too many instances. Note: In examining the issue of *extra* clothing, I find an unusual amount charged the soldier, particularly of boots and shoes. This may be ascribed to losses occasioned by the character of the fatigue service that is done. He who is frequently at work upon roads or employed in boating along rivers must wear out more clothes than he who has no further exposure than guard mounting. Something ought to be done in the case.

²Located at Philadelphia.

58

A soldier should not be required to do severe duty and to pay for it too in the loss of his clothes.

Fort Leavenworth, August 15, 1831
   Clothing. Well marked. I would here again state (as I have often before in previous reports) that very many of the pantaloons issued to the soldiers are too small and short. In truth, with but few exceptions to the contrary, the men of 6 feet high have to compromise the matter between the coat and stockings in the arrangement of the pantaloons, which if properly drawn up shew the leg above the stocking and if not so drawn up expose some portion of the shirt between the waistband and the coat.

Fort Crawford, August 20, 1838
   Clothing. Well marked. I would again express my regret that a change was made in the uniform of 1812—the war uniform. The present coat of the Infantry and Artillery is particularly objectionable, and the color of the cloth pantaloons is by no means the best for service, and it is besides more expensive than the plain blue, which is found at every retail store, as is not the case with the light blue, which very often on the frontier is not to be had at all or at an extravagant price.

Buffalo, October 1, 1838
   None of the companies are in full uniform; in truth, very many of the men are but clad in old fatigue dresses, much patched. The clothing for Company G has arrived, it is said. This I believe to be the case, but at what time the clothing of the other companies may be received is in the highest degree problematical.

I must again repeat that the present system of clothing is bad, and to prove that it is so, one need only read the regulations on the subject, which are no more suited to the exigencies of our service than to those of China.

Fort Crawford, July 11, 1842

The clothing is properly marked, and pains are taken to teach the soldier how to pack it in his knapsack, a lesson not generally attended to as it should be. The coats of the rank and file are unsuitable and ill looking and besides are in some instances made of bad materials, so rotten indeed that in some cases they have become unserviceable after a few days' wear. Restore, if it can be done, the old uniform, the short coat. The long tail of the present coat is an useless appendage and a ridiculous looking one, too, when its wearer is fully equipped with his knapsack and accoutrements. Dispense too with the wings, for they serve only to render less frequent the wearing of the knapsack on drill parades, as the putting of them on and off sadly ruffles or tears the wing. I may at a future time say something on the subject of the uniform of the officer, for it not only is worse than it was before the adoption of the present dress, but it is positively obnoxious to the taste of our people, which condemns want of adaptiveness in every thing.

Fort Atkinson, July 27, 1842

I have heard no complaints of the badness of the material of which the coats are made (as was the case at Fort Crawford) and may therefore take for granted that it is good, which is more than can be said of the cut of the coat itself, which seems not to have been designed for any particular person or so put together as to admit of such alterations as might bring it to the shape of the soldier to whose lot it might fall. The pantaloons are much after the same manner, but this is not so material, as their defects are not so likely to attract notice.

Fort Leavenworth, August 16, 1842

The Infantry company appeared on review in full uniform, the abominable long tail coat with wings, but afterwards in the round blue jacket and white pantaloons, in which it showed to great advantage, as might have been expected under the circumstances of so strong and immediate a contrast.

Fort Leavenworth, August, 1843

The Dragoons are dressed in the prescribed uniform, which (to say nothing about its suitableness) is kept in neat condition. It is wished that the white cotton pantaloons should give place to some dark woolen or other stuff. The present white is so easily soiled that in 10 minutes after the men are mounted, it becomes, by the rubbing of the horses against each other, so stained as to become offensive to the sight, besides which it is totally unfit for use upon the long and frequent excursions over this prairie region, where the dews are heavy during the warm months. In proof, Captain [Philip St. George] Cooke, upon his late excursion towards Santa Fé, took with him no other than woolen pantaloons, and although he has just drawn his summer clothing, he will leave it all behind and take with him the woolen upon his second expedition to escort the Santa Fé traders, which may be expected to depart about the 25th instant. But this order or purpose of his, although necessary, can not be carried into effect without imposing upon the men the cost of the woolens, which must be charged to them as extra. Is there fairness in this?

61

The company of the 1st Infantry appeared to as much advantage in the full uniform as could be expected from such a dress. The two companies of the 3rd, having only within the last 12 hours received its clothing for the year, was fortunately compelled to pass in review in its becoming undress, white pantaloons and round woolen jacket. Throughout the several companies, Dragoon as well as Infantry, the clothing is properly marked, and the clothing itself is of good material and properly made; with regard to this latter assurance I am the more positive, having made an examination under a proper regard to the charge which you gave me some months ago to direct my attention particularly to the clothing, as you had had reports in proof of its being made of inferior and bad materials.

New Orleans Barracks, May 6, 1844

I have seldom seen soldiers more neatly and to all appearance better dressed, but with many it is only in appearance, for their coats, although but a short time in use, are already worn out or torn in many places, so rotten is the cloth. The red coat of the musician is not only of rotten but of badly dyed cloth. Every article is properly marked.

Fort Snelling, August 6, 1845

The clothing fits well and looks particularly clean and neat. The uniform cap is much complained of on account of its weight and unsightly shape, and with reason. The knapsacks are the same that I remarked upon, and not favorably, two years ago, but they may be made to serve their full term. Great coat straps have been recently received, the first that I have seen. They will prove a convenience. At all events the good soldier can now with the straps confine his coat to the smallest possible roll without resorting to the needle and thread as hitherto, a most inconvenient mode, though one often used as a shift by soldiers of another description, who would palm off upon an inspecting officer a sham for the reality. Every article is marked in the manner prescribed by regulation.

MESS

The soldiers at the western posts ate well, according to the simple standards of the day. If there was any one thing which met the almost universal approval of Croghan, it was the garrison messes. He made a special point to inspect them, and he came away with high praise for the variety and quality of the meals and for the care with which the food was served.

What the soldiers got to eat depended primarily upon the subsistence ration allowed each man by law. According to an act of 1802, the fundamental daily ration consisted of one and one-quarter pounds of beef or three-quarters of a pound of pork, eighteen ounces of bread or flour, and one gill of rum, whiskey, or brandy. To this were added, for every hundred rations, two quarts of salt and four quarts of vinegar. Because of dissatisfaction with this fare during the War of 1812, steps were taken to improve it. In 1818 the Secretary of War increased the vegetable part of the ration and directed that twice a week a half-allowance of meat be supplemented by a suitable quantity of peas or beans. Twice a week fresh meat was to be substituted for salted. In 1830 ardent spirits were removed from the ration, and in 1832 allowances of sugar and coffee were issued instead.[3]

The soldiers would have led a rather sad gastronomic existence if they had been limited to these solitary items, yet it must be remembered that officially this was supposed to suffice. "Bread and soup," announced the *General Regulations*, "are

[3] *United States Statutes at Large*, II, 134, 672; III, 427; V, 258–59. See also footnote 2 in chapter V below.

the great items of a soldier's diet in every situation."[4] Luckily, however, the monotony was broken by the garden truck which most garrisons were able to provide for themselves. It will be noted how consistently Croghan cited this as the one factor making or breaking the mess.

The army in Croghan's day had no professional cooks. *Regulations* provided that messes be prepared by "privates of squads, including private musicians, each taking his tour." And detailed instructions for the making of soup and for the baking of bread are set forth in solemn tones.[5] Officers were sternly charged to make the inspection and care of the mess one of their principal duties and were recommended to "read the articles 'Baking,' and 'Bread,' in the different Encyclopaedias." Care for cleanliness in kitchen and utensils was especially enjoined.

Croghan's laudatory statements clearly indicate that this segment of army life was studiously attended to.

Fort St. Philip, June, 1827

Preparation of the men's messes. Care seems to be taken,

---

[4] Paragraph 196, *General Regulations for the Army,* 1825.

[5] The following paragraphs from the *General Regulations for the Army,* 1825, indicate some of the details enjoined upon the officers and cooks:

201. Bread ought not to be burnt, but baked to an equal brown colour. The crust ought not to be detached from the crum. On opening it, when fresh, one ought to smell a sweet and balsamic odour.

202. The troops ought not to be allowed to eat soft bread fresh from the oven, without first toasting it. This process renders it nearly as wholesome and nutritious as stale bread.

203. Fresh meat ought not to be cooked before it has had time to bleed and to cool; and meats will generally be *boiled,* with a view to soup; sometimes roasted or baked, but never *fried.* . . .

205. To make soup, put into the vessel at the rate of five pints of water to a pound of fresh meat; apply a quick heat, to make it boil promptly; skim off the foam, and then moderate the fire; salt is then put in, according to the palate. Add the vegetables of the season one or two hours, and sliced bread some minutes before the simmering is ended. When the broth is sensibly reduced in quantity, that is, after five or six hours' cooking, the process will be complete.

to make the best of that which is furnished by the government, but the fare is not so good as at some other posts. The company is as yet without a garden, a great desideratum everywhere and particularly so in a climate like this. There was once a good garden here, during the command of Major [Enoch] Humphreys. Why it has been permitted to go to waste since his death I know not.

Baton Rouge, May 9, 1829

The soldiers of this garrison live as well as they can desire, far better, I venture to aver, than they were accustomed to prior to enlistment, not only as it may relate to the quality and variety of the dishes served up but also as to the style of the cookery and the order and neatness in which they are presented. And this remark may be applied with like propriety to all our other posts. At some, it is true, they live better than at others from the circumstance of having a greater variety for the kitchen; still the same attention towards having all that can be obtained properly prepared and arranged obtains throughout.

Fort Howard, August 2, 1834

The fare is better here than at either of the two posts just visited [Forts Brady and Mackinac], because a greater variety for the table can be procured and without trouble than can be obtained at those posts upon any terms. Of vegetables there is every kind in abundance, and of a quality superior to any that I have ever before seen. As a vegetable garden General [George M.] Brooke's is perhaps equal to any other in the country north of the 40° N. latitude.

Note. Besides General Brooke's, there is a separate garden belonging to each particular company. The arrangement I

65

like not and would fain hope that an order may be issued ere long prohibiting company officers from employing at will soldiers in gardening or any other work during the intervals of garrison duty. Let every work be performed by regular detail and for the common good, and it will very soon be made to appear that the soldier's fatigue service will be lessened by one half at least.

Fort Snelling, August 16, 1838

No soldiers ought to desire to live better than they have always done at this post. The government ration is sufficient of itself, and to it may be added the abundant supply of vegetables at all times to be had from the gardens of the several companies.

Fort Brady, September 12, 1838

The garrison of this post does not live so well as the garrison of many other places, as it can not draw from its gardens any variety of vegetables—potatoes and cabbages alone being grown, and of these there is now a want. But there is no cause of complaint; on the contrary, perhaps perfect satisfaction, in being sensible that there is not a soldier who does not fare better than the citizens of the village. The command just now labours under a disadvantage owing to the smallness of its numerical force. The beef cattle, being all large, one half at least of every one slaughtered must be salted, and in this way the command is deprived of one half its proper allowance of fresh meat.

Fort Winnebago, July 5, 1842

Here as at all the other posts of the country the subject of men's messes is studiously cared for, and an order and neatness are observed in the kitchen and mess room that would be creditable in any situation. At some posts the fare is better than at others, but it is only that they have better gardens (which are not to be had at every post) or are located where fish and game are abundant.

Fort Leavenworth, August, 1843

The fare is not so good now as it was last year, but only because there is not so abundant a supply of vegetables. It is but seldom indeed, if ever of late, that complaints can be made of soldiers' messing, and if the general belief of the citizens about the several posts be received as correct, they live rather too well.

Fort Crawford, September 11, 1843

Few or none of the families in Prairie du Chien live as well as the soldiers of this garrison or can boast of so great a variety of vegetables. Certainly none can exhibit more neatness or better cookery.

Fort Pike, April 12, 1844

The only difference that I have of late years remarked in the soldiers' fare has been in the greater amount and variety of game, fish, and vegetables that some forts furnish over others not so favorably situated, for at all of them the same pains are taken in the preparation of the different meals, and in no case have I found a want of due attention to cleanliness. Here the kitchen and its utensils, the mess room, and mess furniture are in good condition, and although the dinners may not be so sumptuous as at some other posts, they are still abundant and as good as a soldier ought to desire, better by far than the labouring classes in any of our states are accustomed to.

67

Captain Lee is anxious that sour kraut should be issued to his company in lieu of rice, and it might be well to comply with his wish, as it is a valuable article of diet in all southern climates, being high anti-scorbutic.

New Orleans Barracks, May 6, 1844

There is perhaps no post in the country at which the soldiers live better. They have a pretty good garden of their own, besides which they have hourly opportunities for exchanging with the market people their rations of rice, salt beef, or pork for every variety of vegetables and fruits that they may desire. The companies, even living as they do, contrive to save out of their regular ration allowance $30 each per month on an average. Here for the first time I have found that salt beef is preferred to pork and that the latter is but seldom issued and then in small quantities. The mess rooms and kitchens are as clean and neat as any one could desire.

Fort Washita, June 19, 1844

The post gardens furnish a variety and abundance of fine vegetables and thus it happens that the fare is better at this than at most other posts, for as equal pains are taken throughout, the fare is better at one place than another only as it may have a greater abundance of vegetables. The kitchens and mess rooms are kept in good order, but having dirt floors, they can not be made to look very neatly. One of the companies, G, spreads its table under a shed, which I take for granted will be boarded up before the cold weather sets in.

HOSPITALS AND MEDICAL CARE

Army units were adequately provided with medical services. Almost without exception the frontier forts which Croghan visited were staffed by a surgeon or assistant surgeon, and the hospitals which they maintained and the care they gave the soldiers were highly praised by the Inspector General. The hospital was a regular part of the garrison landscape. Although the buildings often left much to be desired in the way of sturdy construction, the cleanliness with which they were kept and the solicitude shown by the surgeons for the soldiers' health counterbalanced the deficiencies.

Health at the posts seems to have been good, and Croghan seldom found the hospitals filled. Often he reported some cases of dysentery or intermittent fever, regular disturbances among the soldiers in those days, but little of a more serious nature. The good conditions he attributed to the healthful climate and to the care given by the medical officers.

Fort Mackinac, July 14, 1826

Hospital—in all that depends upon the surgeon of the post, arranged and systematized so as to meet the spirit of the regulations as nearly as it may admit. Medical stores and medicines good and in sufficient amount, with the exception of an entire want of a case of surgical instruments (for which a return was forwarded twelve months ago). The building itself, a perfect barn in ruins and so open at the top that during a rain the bunks of the patients are moved about from place to place to avoid the wet—the other rooms under this roof are equally favored. No repairs can be made, the commanding officer having neither the means nor the authority to fasten a shingle.

Fort St. Philip, June, 1827

Hospital—the building too small, it may be said, not at all suited for the purpose. Its location, however, on the banks of the bayou is thought to be a good one. The medical superintendent is a citizen surgeon, who attends likewise upon the sick at Fort Jackson. He is said not to neglect his duty, and that he has skill in his profession can not be questioned, as his services could not be engaged at a less price than a $150 per month. I can not but express my surprise that an army physician can not be spared to this post, especially when the charges of a citizen are so very extravagant.

Jefferson Barracks, September, 1827

The army is truly fortunate in having such a medical corps. At every post that I have visited since my appointment as Inspector General, I have found every thing to admire in this department. More than once I have questioned myself, how it could be that the government were enabled to employ such professional worth and talents at so *paltry* a price.[6]

Fort Howard, June, 1828

Hospital. The building wants some repairs and alterations to render it secure against rain and more convenient. Assistant Surgeon [William] Beaumont acts (as is invariably the case with the officers of the Medical Department) with an exclusive eye to the comfort of the sick.

In looking through the several rooms, my attention was called to the medical library, which as to number of volumes appears well enough but furnishes very little variety. The catalogue stands thus: Bell on venereal 7 copies, Cooper's Surgery 3 ditto, Dispensatory 7 ditto, Dorsey's Cooper 2 ditto, Rush Sydenham 1 ditto, Rush's Pringle 1 ditto, Surgeon's Vade Mecum 8 ditto, and Thomas's Practice 4 ditto.[7]

---

[6] According to *General Regulations for the Army,* 1835, a surgeon received $50 a month plus eight rations, an assistant surgeon, $40 and eight rations.

[7] Croghan lists the medical works informally by what were undoubtedly

In addition to the few standard works now furnished, the best medical journals and most approved treatises on mineralogy and botany are much wanted at all the frontier posts. The first, that it may be in the power of the insulated medical gentlemen to keep pace with the improvements and discoveries that are daily taking place in the science of medicine, the latter as books of reference (without which Mitchell[8] himself would be frequently at fault) to enable them to report with confidence and correctly upon the mineralogical and botanical wealth of their several districts. I submit it to the Surgeon General whether or not the government could be a loser by even the most liberal appropriation towards this purpose.

Of surgical instruments, to include amputating, trepanning, and the pockets, there are perhaps one dozen sets, not one of which is fit for use in the opinion of Assistant Surgeon Beaumont, who looked over them with me. (By an order

their commonly accepted designations. Full titles for those that can be identified are the following:

Benjamin Bell, *A Treatise on Gonorrhea Virulenta, and Lues Venera. With Notes, Adapted to the Present State of Practice of Those Diseases* (Albany, 1814).

Sir Astley Paston Cooper, *The Lectures of Sir Astley Cooper . . . on the Principles and Practice of Surgery; with Additional Notes and Cases* (Boston, 1825–28).

Thomas Sydenham, *The Works of Thomas Sydenham, M.D., on Acute and Chronic Diseases; with Their Histories and Modes of Cure. With Notes, Intended to Accommodate Them to the Present State of Medicine, and to the Climate and Diseases of the United States, by Benjamin Rush* (Philadelphia, 1809).

Sir John Pringle, *Observations on the Diseases of the Army, by Sir John Pringle, bart . . . with Notes, by Benjamin Rush* (Philadelphia, 1810).

Robert Thomas, *The Modern Practice of Physic, Exhibiting the Characters, Causes, Symptoms, Prognostics, Morbid Appearances, and Improved Method of Treating Diseases of All Climates* (New York, 1817).

[8] Probably Samuel Latham Mitchell (1764–1831), a prominent promoter of science and editor of the *Medical Repository*.

from the head of the Department they will be sent to New York for repairs.) An idea has been suggested to me, which if carried into effect might save the government a portion of the present expence in furnishing instruments and besides many an unfortunate the added torture of a dull knife. "Let every surgeon and assistant surgeon be furnished by the government with complete sets of instruments for his own use exclusively during his continuance in service and for which he shall be held individually responsible." Holding his instruments under such a tenure, I am persuaded that there is not a medical gentleman of the army who would not take more care of them (careful though he may now be) than he would of those received after the present mode, of a predecessor to be held for a time and then to be turned over with steward, cook, and all to a successor in office.

Fort Howard, September 28, 1833

Cases in hospital 11, chiefly remittent fevers. This post and the country immediately about it are becoming more unhealthy every year, and cases of fever do now occur of a character such as did not formerly make their appearance. This is ascribable to the draining of the marshes in the rear of the fort, by which a large surface of vegetable matter in a state of decomposition is left exposed and free to emit its poisonous effluvia.

Fort Brady, September 12, 1838

Fortunately there are no sick at the post, else there would be much distress, as there is no medical gentleman, either military or civil, nearer than Mackinac. It is earnestly hoped that the garrison will not long remain without someone to take charge of its hospital.

Fort Leavenworth, July, 1840

Hospital. Surgeon [Edward] Macomb. There is perhaps not a better hospital of its size in the country. I am certain not a more attentive physician than the gentleman who has charge of it. This post has never been severely visited by sickness since its first establishment in 1827. At present there are but few in hospital and a portion of those from casualties. No department of our service is entitled to more, if so much, credit as the medical; each of its officers would seem to vie with his fellows in his attentions to the sick, and aware of this the soldier, who but a few years back had a perfect horror of the hospital, now goes to it when sick, assured that all that care and skill can do will be done to effect his speedy cure.

Fort Crawford, September, 1840

There has been much sickness at the post during the last two months, and I regret to state that there are at this time about 40 on the sick report. The number of cases is, however, diminishing. The prevailing diseases have been dysentery and intermittent fever. The hospital is not built after the most approved plan; still it is not illy arranged, and its wards and store rooms are kept in much neater order than they were in 1838. Owing to the very many cases of intermittent fever, the supply of quinine has been exhausted. Dr. [Alfred W.] Elwes can, however, at any time be furnished from Galena. The wall and paling enclosing the hospital garden are rather decayed and dilapidated and ought (for appearance' sake if nothing else) to be repaired, for they form the only exceptions to the fine condition of every thing appertaining to Fort Crawford.

Fort Winnebago, July 5, 1842

Assistant Surgeon [Charles H.] Laub has but three cases in hospital, none of them severe. This department, in whatever may relate to it, is conducted with such invariable efficiency and adeptness that for years past I have inspected the post hospitals as much from inclination as duty, confident that I should meet much [to] gratify and nothing to dissatisfy me. It is not now as it once was when soldiers abhorred the very idea of being sent to the hospital, and not without cause. Now they go to it without apprehension and in the full assurance that all the comforts that they may stand in need of will be afforded to them and that medical skill and attention will be at work to effect their cure. Dr. Laub reports a sufficiency of whatever he may stand in need of until the arrival of the medicines and stores estimated for some months ago.

Fort Atkinson, September 7, 1843

The hospital is well arranged, the ward rooms are of proper size, well ventilated, and in every respect better than are usually met with at so small a fort. The number of sick is small, and in truth such is the healthfulness of the place that but for the casualties which are always occurring at Dragoon posts to a greater or less extent, the sick reports would not average two per day. Dr. King, the only medical officer at the post, is most favorably spoken of by everyone.

Fort Crawford, September 11, 1843

I have not yet visited a hospital that was not kept in admirable order, but this more than all other merits unlimited praise, for it is not only in good order but is so positively clean and neat in the ward rooms, kitchens, store rooms, and offices, that not a speck of dirt or even soiled spot is to be detected. There have been a good many sick, but the number is lessening; none of the cases are of a malignant character. It is almost needless to assure you that every patient sent to the hospital finds in Surgeon [Charles] McDougall a most attentive and skillful physician.

Baton Rouge, May 8, 1844
Surgeon [Benjamin F.] Harney seems to pay every attention to the sick, of whom he has at present but 4, none of them seriously indisposed. The hospital appears to be an uncomfortable building, rendered so by its exposed situation, being completely uncovered, without trees or shade of any kind, to the scorching rays of the sun. It is true that a gallery extends entirely around the building, but it does not prevent the sun from shining into the sick wards. I have advised Dr. Harney to endeavour to get an awning for the entire west front. The supply of medicines and medical stores is abundant and of good quality.

Fort Mackinac, August 23, 1845
Assistant Surgeon Byrne has few sick, but the arrangement of the hospital, its neatness, and proper supply of medicines and medical stores give every assurance that, let many patients come when they may, they will find every comfort and that kind and skillful treatment that has robbed our hospitals of the terrors which once surrounded them.

Dr. Byrne has had some of the rooms of the hospital painted at his own expence, having been unable to have it done at the public cost, and he is now endeavouring to create a fund to be appropriated exclusively to such uses by requiring the payment of fifty cents from every citizen who may be either bled or have a tooth drawn by the steward or any of the attendants of the hospital.

CHAPLAINS

In 1838 Congress established regular chaplaincies for the army.[9] Most of the western posts were thus provided with a regular chaplain, whose duties included that of schoolmaster as well as minister of religion. Croghan came into little contact with them, but he noted occasionally the building of chapels for their use and strongly insisted that the expenses be charged to the Quartermaster Department and not to the special funds provided by the councils of administration.

Jefferson Barracks, August 27, 1843

A very neat chapel has been erected under the superintendence of Captain [Bradford R.] Alden and is so nearly finished that service is regularly held in it by the chaplain of the post, the Reverend Mr. Hedges of the Episcopal Church.

Chaplains being authorized by the law and with regularly appointed duties, everything necessary to the proper performance of those duties should be provided at the public expence. A chapel and school room then being necessary, they ought to be built in the same way with other public buildings and not by a call upon private funds, as is like to be the case in the present instance.

It is true that the material of one of the public stables has been given by the Quartermaster Department for its erection, but much more will be needed before completion, let Captain Alden be as economical as he may.

Three hundred dollars must be provided to pay present debts and meet future claims; let them be drawn from the

[9] *United States Statutes at Large,* V, 259; General Orders No. 29, War Department, Adjutant General's Office, August 18, 1838.

Quartermaster General, not from the council of administration, which properly has as little to do with the building of churches or chapels as with the erection of magazines or hospitals.

Fort Gibson, July 1, 1844

Lieutenant Colonel [Gustavus] Loomis, the late commandant (now on furlough), has caused to be built out of materials prepared by the assistant quartermaster for other and public purposes a house to be used as a school room and chapel. I regret that the Lieutenant Colonel thought proper to direct such an expenditure, as he will be held individually liable for its amount, and I the more regret it as such a building was not required, there being vacant rooms enough for the school and for a chapel too whenever a chaplain shall be appointed.

POST RECORDS

The army, of course, could not get along without considerable record keeping, and many types of record books were prescribed. The *General Regulations* of 1825, for example, lists thirteen separate books which were to be maintained by the army units, including such books as collections of general and regimental orders, descriptive books for officers and enlisted men, letter books, morning reports, registry of furloughs, descriptions of deserters, court-martial records, and registry of deceased soldiers.[10]

Croghan did not take a very keen interest in the details of these records, although each of his reports has a separate section headed "Books." To inspect them carefully in the short time he had at each post was probably a hopeless task because of the lack of uniformity, which the Inspector frequently crit-

[10] Article 36, *General Regulations for the Army*, 1825.

icizes. The regulations, unfortunately, were less than explicit concerning the form. The books, according to the indefinite directives, were to be "of two widths, or 12 inches for the larger size, and about 8½ for the small; and of two lengths, or 17½ inches for the first, and 13 inches for the other. Each book will contain a quantity of paper, according to destination."[11] That left a good deal of room for the interpretation and taste of the officer concerned, and Croghan pleaded for exact forms with the headings and lines properly ruled off.

Fort Snelling, August, 1826

Books—correctly kept, it is believed, but differently perhaps from the form intended by the framers of the regulation. I would have it understood that the regimental books and such company books as have been exhibited are to the fullest sense of the term the property of the regiment, not having been furnished by the Quartermaster Department but made at the post out of such paper suited to the purpose as could be purchased of the sutler. I have seen no reason as yet to doubt the great desire of the several officers whom I have visited to procure books of the size and form prescribed and to keep them after the manner intended by the regulations, but as yet few have been received, and as they came on without being headed, each receiver of a set was left to follow his own understanding of the expression of the regulations, which, unfortunately for the convenience of the inspecting officers, led him to mark out forms widely different from those fixed upon by anyone else. To remedy this inconvenience new sets of books should be furnished so soon as practicable to every company and regiment, accompanied by printed forms of the manner of entry for each particular book, so precisely drawn

11 *Ibid.*, Paragraph 283.

that to mistake would be impossible unless by willful negligence. I believe truly that there is not a colonel or captain in the service who would not willingly pay himself for such books, sooner than have the correctness of his present mode of keeping accounts so frequently called in question.

Fort Snelling, August 17, 1834

None of the books, I am sure, exhibit incorrect entries, but the books of no two companies are kept after the same form. Some of them too have occasionally been kept by bad scribes, for it sometimes happens that a company can not furnish even one tolerable clerk.

Fort Snelling, August 16, 1838

Books. Correctly kept it is believed so far as the propriety of entries are concerned, but not agreeably to the same or to any particular forms, as must and will continue to be the case so long as company officers are left to give their own reading to the regulation on the subject, which, by the by, is neither sufficiently explicit nor satisfactory.

Fort Crawford, September, 1840

Books. Correctly kept; and here let me suggest the propriety of having all regiment and company books that may hereafter be issued ruled off and leaded precisely alike if it be considered of consequence that the same forms of entry be adopted throughout, for the present regulation on the subject is so worded as to admit of various constructions and of course to as many different forms of record.

Fort Washita, June 19, 1844

Books. Correctly kept but not in every instance neatly.

It sometimes happens that none of the non-commissioned officers of a company are competent to perform the duties of clerk, and regrets that it should be so are often expressed at many of our posts. There is no excuse in this, however, for want of neatness (I allude not to this post particularly), as the company commandants can require the assistance of their subalterns, but such has not been the custom. Commandants of companies either keep the books themselves or intrust them to their orderly sergeants. Many years ago Captain [Samuel] Spotts, then of the Artillery, arrested and brought to trial one of his subalterns for refusing to assist him in keeping the company books. The sentence, if I mistake not, was "to be publicly reprimanded," thus virtually declaring that subalterns are bound when called upon by the company commandant to perform any company duty whatsoever.

4: SUPPLIES AND EQUIPMENT

O F GREAT CONCERN to army officials in Washington was the equipping of the western forts, and the Inspector General was responsible for transmitting to them an independent appraisal of the system of supply on the frontier. Croghan accepted this charge seriously; substantial sections of his reports deal with the important but largely uninteresting question of equipment in the hands of the troops.

The supply of the forts was broken down officially into various classes, each under a separate staff division. The distinct types of supplies usually were given distinct sections in the annual reports of the tours of inspection—quartermaster supplies, subsistence stores, ordnance equipment. For things not supplied by the government, the soldiers were forced to depend upon the civilian sutlers. Croghan included these men, too, in his reports.

QUARTERMASTER AND SUBSISTENCE SUPPLIES

The largest elements in the supplying of the frontier posts were the goods purchased by the Quartermaster General and the Commissary General of Subsistence.[1] The subsistence stores

[1] The Quartermaster Department and the Office of Commissary General of Subsistence were organized in 1818. *United States Statutes at Large,* III, 426–27. Their respective duties are set forth in the *General Regulations for the Army.* See Lurton D. Ingersoll, *A History of the War Department of the United States, with Biographical Sketches of the Secretaries* (Washington, 1879), for a discussion of these staff offices.

were contracted for on the basis of sealed bids, usually with individual contracts for each post. Contractors in the eastern cities agreed to deliver at a certain date the salt pork, the beans, and the minor items which made up the basic ration. The fresh beef called for by the ration was of necessity supplied by farmers close at hand. With the exception of a few medical supplies and the necessary ordnance, everything else needed for the maintaining of the forts fell in the province of the quartermaster.

The quartermaster officer at any frontier fort was a busy man. He had to build and maintain the barracks and fortifications (often with only the skill he could find among the troops). He had to procure the fuel and forage needed by the garrison, and to him fell the responsibilities for transportation of troops and supplies. And when the War Department attempted to make the forts more self-sufficient by instituting an extensive farming program, it was the quartermaster again who bore the brunt of the burden. At small posts—and that meant most of the western ones—the quartermaster officer was also the subsistence officer, and other odd assignments might fall his way.

Croghan came in close contact with the quartermaster officers, and his reports are nearly always sympathetic. He inspected the stores of food and other supplies, checked the condition of the storehouses, investigated the fulfillment of contracts, and noted special difficulties from post to post. His criticisms are leveled more against the system of supplying and maintaining stores than against any individual officer, whose impossible tasks he understood.

Fort Crawford, October 11, 1836

The expence of fire wood at this post would be lessened 50 per centum were it furnished by private contract. In issuing proposals to furnish agreeably to the usual mode, conspiracies are sure to be formed whereby the government becomes much the loser. Proposals are never handed in by more than one person, but he is the representative of some half dozen of his neighbours, equally interested with himself in the price which is to be obtained because they are to be equal sharers in the profits of the contract.

Fort Des Moines, October 26, 1836

There are many articles borne upon the returns and in store which are worn out and much in the way, such as old camp kettles and mess pans, hoes with nothing left but the eye, spades without blades, etc., etc. There ought to be a fixed time for dropping such trash. When Fort Armstrong was broken up, many articles belonging to this as well as to the ordnance department were shipped to St. Louis which, if sold, would not have paid the cost of transportation, and for no other reason than that being noted on the returns the officers having charge of them would have been held accountable in case of their loss or damage.

Fort Leavenworth, 1838

The experiment which is now being made under instructions from the Department of War to grow at this post the requisite forage for the horses and cattle belonging to the proper garrison of the place (and which cannot fail of complete success) will prove to have decided advantages over the present system of supplies by contract, first on the score of economy and again in the assurance which it holds out of a more certain and liberal provision. About 1,000 acres of prairie are now under fence and in corn, from which 20,000 bushels may be expected, that is to say, 20 bushels an acre or half a crop and no more, such being the average of prairie lands that have been broken up during the fall previous to planting. It is intended, I believe, to plant this field in corn

83

next spring; should this be the case and the season not prove particularly unfavorable, a crop of 40 bushels to the acre at the least will be gathered in.

The average contract price of corn on delivery here for several years past has not been less than 50 cents a bushel—a cost far exceeding all the expences that can attend its procurement under the system now about to go into operation. Thirty men—practical farmers—are, it is believed, fully competent to the cultivation of 1,000 acres of good prairie land, provided that the assistance of the soldiers of the garrison be granted them during seed time and harvest, and thirty men can be had for $20 each per month, inclusive of a ration a day. That is to say, the entire yearly cost of the hired labourers would be but $7,200, an amount by no means equal to half the sum that the product of their labour would command, taking the contract prices as the standard for determining its value.

For the cultivation above stated, thirty horses and a like number of ploughs and harnesses would be necessary, but the expence attending their procurement would not in the first instance exceed $3,000, and in each succeeding year $800 would be found fully enough to supply any losses that might have occurred either in horses or farming utensils, particularly as the condemned Dragoon horses could be turned over to the Quartermaster Department for plough horses and the farming utensils might be renewed with little cost by the artificer of the post. In estimating the proceeds of the labour of thirty men, which may be rated at $20,000 a year, I have not included the value of the fodder, pumpkins, and pease, cultivated and gathered in with the crop of corn, which may be fairly stated at $3,000 or as equal to the original cost of the horses, ploughs, etc., employed in the cultivation.

84

In this statement the 30 labourers have been assigned exclusively to the cultivation of corn or nearly so; but they might also attend to a crop of 500 acres of oats and as many acres of meadow as might be found necessary to enclose (reference being had to the amount of other provender raised), and that too without interrupting the necessary cultivation of the corn crop, provided always that the necessary assistance be afforded by the soldiery during seed time and harvest. Let us assume that the daily issue of forage at this post is to 500 horses, the yearly consumption will then be about 45,000 bushels of corn and 1,100 tons of hay—the cost of which at the average contract prices, corn at 50 cents a bushel and hay at $6.00 for a ton, would be $29,650 or $20,000 more than all the expenditure attendant upon its procurement through the means of hired labour.

Fort Snelling, August 16, 1838
Supplies fully sufficient for the subsistence of a garrison of two hundred men until June next, or until the delivery of the next contract. Every part of the ration is good, vinegar excepted, which, by the by, is not often of good quality.

Fort Brady, September 12, 1838
Quartermaster's Department. Lieutenant [William] Root. The supply on hand equal to the wants of the post. There is here as at almost every other post a large amount of unserviceable articles that ought to be so disposed of as to relieve the officer of all further care of them—they serve but to lumber up the store rooms.
Subsistence Department. The provisions in store are of good quality and sufficient for the purposes of a much larger command until the close of the next summer.

85

Fort Leavenworth, July, 1840

Quartermaster Department. Captain [Thomas] Swords. The duties devolved upon this officer are, if not arduous, at least sufficiently composite to afford him full employment. He has just returned from an inspection of the military road leading from this post [to] the Arkansas, over which he has supervision and which is very nearly finished, agreeably to the contract. The Captain has in cultivation a field of about 800 acres in corn, oats, and timothy, which promises fairly. When the harvest is gathered in, an estimate of costs may be made out from which a correct decision can be drawn as to the propriety of continuing this system of cultivation.

Fort Snelling, July 16, 1842

The supply of subsistence is abundant, of the best quality, and stored with every care to its preservation.

The saw mill at the Falls is now being put in complete order and at an expence, when compared with the pecuniary gain or rather saving that will be derived from it, quite trifling.[2] Repairs must absolutely be made because necessary to the preservation of some of the buildings, and they can be completed very soon after the mill is in operation and without any material expenditure of money, as the chief cost or trouble in the erection or repairs of buildings at this post have always been in the procurement of lumber, which will now be furnished by the mill. Lieutenant [Ferdinand S.] Mumford seems fully sensible of the necessity for the exercise of a rigid economy, and I feel every assurance that he will undertake only such repairs as are absolutely necessary and will hasten

2 The sawmill at the Falls of St. Anthony, on the Mississippi at the present site of Minneapolis, was built by the soldiers of Fort Snelling in 1821. Edward A. Bromley, "The Old Government Mills at the Falls of St. Anthony," *Minnesota Historical Collections*, X, part 2, 635–43.

their completion with as little call upon the funds of his department as possible. It is needless that I should specify the various repairs necessary, as you are doubtless in possession of a particular report on the subject, made some two years ago by the quartermaster of the post by order of the Quartermaster General. I only have to express a hope that the assistant quartermaster, Lieutenant Mumford, may be left to the exercise of his own sound judgment in the matter.

Fort Atkinson, July 27, 1842

The flour is not good; at all events the post baker, an experienced man in his line, assures me that he can not make good bread without mixing some of the old flour with the new, that is, last year's flour with the present. The barrels, if not before in use, are certainly badly made and quite shattered. It is thought that on an average twenty pounds of flour in each barrel is caked on the outside and sour from exposure to the weather, either before or after its delivery on the bank of the Mississippi. The pork is even in a worse condition than the flour; some of it is quite soft and nearly unfit for use, and in many barrels it is rusty throughout. Lieutenant [Fowler] Hamilton has more than once poured fresh brine into the barrels, but they are so open that it very soon ran out. The fear is that long before the next delivery much of the flour and most of the pork must be condemned as unfit for issue.

Both the flour and pork are under Atchison's contract, and the belief is that neither was properly inspected.[3] Mr. Bass,

[3] John Atchison of Galena, Illinois, won the 1842 contract for supply of subsistence goods at Fort Crawford. The contract, which apparently included the goods for Fort Atkinson also, called for 600 barrels of pork, 1,200 barrels of flour, 540 bushels of white field beans, 9,000 pounds of soap, 600 pounds of candles, 180 bushels of salt, and 2,400 gallons of vinegar. Copies of Contracts (1838–42), Subsistence Department, National Archives.

the contractor to transport the provisions, etc., to this place from the Mississippi, roundly asserts that McGregor of Prairie du Chien (a regular inspector of the Territory), never examined a barrel of the pork, although he certified that he had inspected every barrel carefully. The fellow ought to be prosecuted.

Fort Leavenworth, August 16, 1842

Contracts have been entered into for the furnishing of fire wood and the necessary forage and upon terms far from unfavorable, viz., wood at $2.49 the cord, hay $3.71 the ton, and corn 34½ cents the bushel. The farm is still kept up, but as yet without profit, nor need profit ever be expected so long as it is cultivated by soldiers and under the direction of a military officer, ignorant (as most officers are) of even the first principles of farming. There are a few hired citizens at work on the farm, but they can scarce be reckoned at all among the number that are called out of the several companies for duty there. The entire number of citizens in the employ of the department is only fourteen, whether as teamsters, blacksmiths, or farmers. Some hay, corn, and oats will be gathered in from the public field this year, but in amount far less than a supply for the post. I would advise that the entire field be put in timothy, for besides that it would furnish all the hay that might be needed (1,000 tons), it would also serve admirably as a pasture for the horses upon their return from the summer's campaign.

Fort Snelling, September 3, 1843

In my last report I spoke confidently of the expected benefit to be derived from the saw mill at the Falls (which was then just completed under the active superintendence of Lieutenant Mumford), but it now appears most unexpectedly and greatly to my surprise that since that time little or nothing has been done. No plank, scantling, or building material of any kind have been cut and this solely because no lumber (saw logs) has been procured, and which can only be done during the winter and early spring months. The late commandant, Major [Greenleaf] Dearborn, has doubtless his reasons and good ones for letting the last winter pass by without securing lumber enough to occupy the mill during the summer and fall, but I regret nevertheless that he was compelled so to act, as the garrison is much reduced since last winter, and consequently the work when undertaken will press the more heavily. (I have expressed my belief to the commandant and other officers, with a view to have them act, that they will be permitted to enlarge and repair their quarters, provided they furnish all the necessary materials for so doing without cost to the public, all of which they can do in the course of the next summer provided a proper supply for the saw mill be secured during the winter.)

The commissary store and such of the officers' quarters as leak badly ought to be reshingled before the winter sets in. I trust therefore that the Quartermaster General will instruct Lieutenant Marston to purchase the necessary number of shingles forthwith. They can be had on the St. Croix, under a contract to deliver them at the post for three dollars a thousand or less, a price less than the cost of getting them by a detail of soldiers, as there is no good timber hereabouts. The procurement of fuel has become a very serious matter and the more since the receipt of the order restricting the wood cutters to the military reserve, which is made up of $\frac{7}{8}$ prairie and $\frac{1}{8}$ wood land.

Fort Pike, April 12, 1844

Subsistence Department. The present small supply was obtained by purchase, but I understand that for the future the supplies (coffee and sugar excepted) will be furnished by a contractor. This I regret, as the cost of provisioning the post will be greatly increased.

Baton Rouge, May 8, 1844

The ration with the exception of sugar and coffee is furnished by contract. The fresh beef, of which one issue only per week is made, is bad, and no better need be expected until the close of the present contract, and even then we have no assurance that a change for the better will be made. A wealthy man in the neighbourhood seems to have the matter exclusively in his own hands; indeed hitherto he has been the only bidder. . . .

I ask that an order be obtained prohibiting officers from sending to the arsenals articles in themselves valueless and irreparable. Hundreds of dollars are yearly paid for the transportation of articles not worth a cent. A short time since, there was brought from Fort Jesup among other trumpery an old table invoiced "laboratory table," a thing that might have been made for three dollars and which perhaps cost five for its transportation. If articles irreparable be condemned at a post, let them be there sold or dropped, thus the cost of transportation at least will be saved.

Fort Smith, June 27, 1844

The supplies for the post are mainly kept in the store house upon the bank of the river immediately above the village of Fort Smith, where they are very unsafe, as they may be easily broken into by anyone so disposed and are furthermore but indifferently protected from the weather. The building is after this wise: posts have been stuck in the ground on which plates are put and upon them the rafters which support the roof, the sides and ends being closed by a weather board of the thinnest sheathing—the floor of earth. Now, as might have been expected, the posts, not being confined by girders or transoms, have been forced outwards by the weight of the roof, which has sunk so much that nothing but very strong braces in aid of the posts prevents it from tumbling in, and should there be a gale of wind or during the coming winter a heavy fall of snow, down it will come. Then as to its security against plunderers (I will not say burglars as there could be no *forcible* entry), a child of five years old could make an entrance in fifteen minutes either by pulling off the weather board or cutting through it with a pen knife.

ORDNANCE

As a military man Croghan took a special interest in the ordnance of the frontier fortresses. He purported to have special competence when it came to examining the guns and ordnance stores, which after all were the basic element in making a post a military installation and not merely a garrison for troops. What he found did not please him. Under this head we get a repetition of his complaint that the forts were not well enough supplied with guns and ammunition and that the men were not adequately trained to use what was on hand. If we were to take at face value the remarks the Inspector General makes about the destitute condition of some of the posts, we would be forced to conclude that they were mere travesties on frontier defense.

Fort St. Philip, June, 1827
There are two pieces (iron sixes) mounted on travelling

91

carriages and complete, and the contents of the arsenal are generally serviceable, but these excepted, almost everything else that can now be brought under view is in a miserable state. The fort itself looks as if it had been for a long time abandoned, the platforms are tumbling in, and the gun carriages are no longer able to sustain the weight of their guns, which are falling from them in every direction. Captain [Samuel] Spotts has but recently taken command here and can not therefore be held responsible for all this, but neglect is justly chargeable somewhere, else more than 40 pieces of ordnance, most of them heavy, would not have been for years exposed without a covering or protection to the inclemencies of the weather, some upon their rotten carriages on the decayed platforms, others upon the glacis of the fort, and perhaps most generally covered with grass and rank growing weeds. The magazine contains about 9,000 pounds of powder, nearly one half of which is cannon and unserviceable. The building is badly suited for the preservation of ammunition of any kind; from want of proper ventilation alone (apart from other objections) it will always be, during the summer months, damp and suffocatingly hot.

Fort Winnebago, August 25, 1838

There is a sufficient supply of powder and fixed ammunition for both cannon and small arms.

Of muskets—there are but barely enough to arm the soldiers of the company. This ought not to be—every frontier post should at all times have such a supply as to enable it to arm all the inhabitants in its neighborhood. The Winnebagoes have of late been very insolent and troublesome, which would not have been the case had they believed that there were muskets enough on hand to furnish one to each of the two hundred labourers now employed on the canal across the portage.

Fort Crawford, September 11, 1843

Since the shipment to St. Louis arsenal of all surplus and unserviceable ordnance and ordnance stores by order of Colonel [Stephen W.] Kearny in September or October last, no material change has been brought about. Nothing worth noting has been received, and but little has been expended beyond the cartridges issued to the guard. The morning and evening guns required by order are not fired, there being too few cartridges in store to warrant the expenditure.

New Orleans Barracks, May 6, 1844

There is a magazine, but there are neither ordnance nor stores. I think that two 6 pounders at least might be furnished for the purpose of firing salutes. Not long since, the governor of the state accompanied by his staff paid a formal visit to the post, when the want of such guns was brought but too forcibly before the commandant.

Fort Jesup, May 14, 1844

There are two iron 6 pounders at the post. The magazine is a pretty good one though badly located. It contains powder only. There should at least be a few prepared cartridges to issue in case of a forward movement. I have not before seen so frontier a post thus destitute.

Fort Washita, June 19, 1844

Each company is well supplied with carbine cartridges, which it keeps in its own store room, there being as yet no magazine. The post possesses two 6 pounders, but has so

93

limited an amount of ammunition that no morning or evening guns can be fired. If I mistake not, the commandant has told me that a requisition went on to Washington with a view to these very morning and evening guns, and received for reply, "Such firing refers more particularly to Artillery posts." Now with all deference I would remark that if the necessity for such practice be determined by the good effects to be produced, one gun here would be of more value than a thousand fired at Fort Columbus or any other of our sea board fortresses.[4] Recollect, this post is upon our extreme Indian frontier and that the wild Indians who sometimes visit it would be forcibly (favorably) struck by the sound of a big gun that can carry a shot far beyond the range of their rifles and very apt to carry back to their own country the most exaggerated accounts of the destruction it can be made to deal forth.

SMALL ARMS AND EQUIPMENT

A special and usually detailed section of each inspection report was the one labeled "Arms and Equipments." Here Croghan set down his observations on the personal arms of the men and the accompanying accouterments—the cartridge boxes, knapsacks, and bayonet scabbards. He checked on the serviceableness of the muskets and carbines, both from the standpoint of their style and manufacture and from the standpoint of the care with which they were maintained by the soldiers. On both counts Croghan was often dissatisfied. He sent detailed objections to the General-in-chief about defects in the style of the weapons. His greatest indignation, however, he reserved for the overzealous care of the soldiers to make things pretty for parade with no concern for the damage done to the pieces by excessive

[4] Fort Columbus was one of the defenses of New York harbor.

polishing and burnishing. It is the practical soldier again who exhibits himself in these remarks.[5]

Fort Crawford, August, 1826

Appearance of the troops under arms—pretty good but without that very minute attention to exterior dress that I have remarked elsewhere. A close inspection shews that every article is clean and that the muskets, although not highly burnished, are in every instance fit for immediate service in the field. Lieutenant Colonel [Willoughby] Morgan would sooner have his command one of usefulness than of shew, and here I would respectfully suggest either that the musket be browned or that less value for the future be put upon its excessive burnish. The soldier, fearing reprimand if he is upon parade without having his musket like a mirror, spares no pains and makes use of every means however improper for having it so. The piece is completely unstocked, and when the business of polishing is over, the ramrod is found bent, perhaps the barrel too, and the trigger guard so sprung as no longer to be brought to its proper place.

Fort Towson, August, 1827

Arms in the hands of the men in the highest possible degree of polish, but throughout unserviceable. They have here, as at Cantonment Jesup, a fashion of staining the stock of the musket with vermillion and also of softening the pan steel, that it may receive the better polish—both these practices

[5] For detailed descriptions of various military arms, see Arcadi Gluckman, *United States Martial Pistols and Revolvers* (Buffalo, 1939), and *United States Muskets, Rifles, and Carbines* (Buffalo, 1948). Berkeley R. Lewis, *Small Arms and Ammunition in the United States Service* (*Smithsonian Miscellaneous Collections,* CXXIX, Washington, 1956), gives valuable information about the small arms and accouterments used by the troops. See also Carl P. Russell, *Guns on the Early Frontiers* (Berkeley, 1957), 142–98.

will be put a stop to. A new supply of arms has been received and will be issued to the companies, but not for daily use; the old muskets are to be retained for garrison purposes.

Jefferson Barracks, August 6, 1831

So far as exterior appearance may be considered, the arms and equipments of both regiments are in as finished order as the most exact care of the soldiers can place them in. The muskets are excessively burnished, and the cartridge boxes and bayonet scabbards are as shining as heel ball and varnish can make them. If their fitness for service be inquired into, they might be pronounced generally serviceable, but if the present mode of cleaning them be persisted in, they will not long remain so.

Under the present order of things, when an officer loses character with the inspecting officers should the muskets of his command shine not like polished steel and the cartridge boxes look like japan itself, neither musket nor box can last longer than 6 or 8 years, unless it be simply for shew. The first will be worn thin and bent from constant rubbing, and the latter will become so stiff that its thick and rotten lid can no longer be lifted up.

Both musket and cartridge box may be made to last 20 years (if originally good) provided the proper mode for preserving them be used, and it is directly the reverse of the one now in vogue.[6]

[6] Croghan's complaints about the care of muskets and cartridge boxes were eventually heeded. In the *General Regulations* issued in 1835 the section on Preservation of Arms and Accoutrements provided: "The arms will not be taken to pieces, without express permission from the Captain or other commissioned officer. The practice of highly polishing the barrels of the muskets will be discontinued; all that need be required is, that they be kept clean and free from rust, except the bayonet and bands, which are to be kept bright. Cartridge-boxes will be polished with blacking instead of varnish, as the latter

Fort Des Moines, October 26, 1836

Lieutenant Colonel [Richard B.] Mason does not consider the patent carbine so efficient an arm as we have all along believed it to be, and in truth other officers of the corps agree in opinion with him. The chief complaint is in the uncertainty of its fire, which on an average does not take place oftener than eight out of twelve trials. I can readily conceive that in the course of a day's march the cartridge, which can not be driven home with any force (the finger only being used), might by its own gravity become so separated from its chamber as to render its ignition doubtful even though the cap should explode; but in the hands of the infantryman, who would at all times carry the barrel of the piece somewhat elevated, this separation could not take place, and thus the chances of ignition would be greatly increased. I have, however, seen the carbine misfire, and at this post, when the cartridge was certainly fully home, thus showing most conclusively that either the cartridge is made of powder too coarse to enter the nipple of the lock or that the nipple itself does not properly connect with the chamber. I will make no further remarks for the present but defer them until I reach Washington, when with carbine in hand I will be enabled to point out its defects in a way more satisfactory to you than I could by a written explanation of them.

Fort Leavenworth, August, 1838

Recently some carbines have been received of different caliber and shorter in the barrel than those first issued, with which some of the men have been furnished, which although shorter than the first are still liable to the material objec-

cannot be used without injury to the leather. *White lead* is forbidden to be used in cleaning the belts and gloves; it being found to possess qualities injurious to health, when near the person."

97

tions urged by me in a former report against all fire arms for Dragoons that load at the breech or are fired by percussion. The pistols are mostly in firing order but are of all patterns from 1812 to the present day, and the same remark may apply to the cartridge boxes, but few of which are serviceable owing to original defects rather than to a want of care in their preservation. The saddle bags are by no means suited to the nature of our Dragoon service; they are not only much too large, but are besides so badly shaped that when packed they cannot be carried on the saddle without greatly inconveniencing both the rider and his horse. The swords are bad, in truth the blades of many of them are entirely unserviceable, being so soft that it may be questioned whether or not the skull of an Indian might not prove too hard for them. I greatly prefer the Dragoon sword of 1812, for from it some service might be expected; apart from the blade of the present sword, the scabbard is too thin and easily indented.

Fort Snelling, August 16, 1838

The muskets, which are of New Haven manufacture of 1831, have been for some years in use, but pains having been taken to preserve them, they are throughout serviceable and in admirable keeping. The cartridge boxes are also in order and serviceable. Of the bayonet scabbards I can only say that they are worth but little, though perhaps as serviceable as when they were new and first issued. The belts are good, but it were better if black ones were substituted in all cases for the white ones now in use. The knapsack is very defective, like all others that I have seen, but in what consists its defects, or rather how they are to be remedied, I dare not venture to declare. I only know that the knapsack hangs badly and causes much annoyance to the soldier.

Fort Brady, September 12, 1838

Arms and equipments. Both look well, for they are clean, but neither can be rated as complete and serviceable. The cartridge boxes might answer, but the muskets are in too many cases defective in the lock to be confidently relied on. Muskets, which have in the course of four years passed through the hands of several different recruits, as has been the case with these, cannot be supposed to escape without most material injury and defacement—let the care of the officer in command be as it may.

Detroit Arsenal, September 27, 1838   *8 50 7 9*

Arms and equipments. Every article under this head was issued but a few weeks since and must be declared serviceable, although none of them can be ranked of the best description. The muskets are of 1822 of Springfield and are like too many of the muskets of that year and of 1825, very defective and coarse. The boxes are made of the very worst of spongy leather.

Fort Leavenworth, July, 1840

The carbine. Even when new a defective arm and now much out of order (those recently received excepted); defective or unsuited to Dragoon service because when carried, as it must be, muzzle downwards, the charge is soon so far separated from its proper chamber as to render its ignition a matter of doubt; after a day's march of 25 or 30 [miles] . . . a loss of fire of ⅖ might be expected. It is also too weak at the small of the stock to bear the rough handling and hard knocks inseparable from this frontier service. Those most out of order seem to be such as the most care and pains have been taken with. Unlike the musket, the carbine requires but

99

little handling. Burnish the musket ever so much, and it will continue serviceable a long time. Not so with the carbine (of the present pattern), for in taking pains to improve its looks you very soon bring about so distinct a separation between the chamber and the barrel of the piece that the powder insinuates itself therein, to the endangering of the person firing and the certain destruction of the piece itself—several instances of the kind have occurred in this command.

Pistols and holsters. Of the holsters and covers I may say in a word that they are much the worse for wear and are looking badly. The pistols are of three different patterns, one of which only is worth anything—viz., the one with a ram rod on a swivel. I am informed by Colonel Kearny that it is thought the Secretary of War intends dispensing with the pistol as part of the Dragoon equipment. I agree in the perfect propriety of such determination, provided a proper carbine be furnished in place of the very defective one now in use —one to load at the muzzle and large enough to chamber three buck shot.

Cartridge boxes and priming or cap boxes. The cartridge boxes last received are the best that I have yet seen and very different in shape from the old ones, many of which are still in use and serviceable. The cap boxes are condemned as unserviceable by all who have used them. They are, too, so shaped that the cap can not be fired unless the piece be at a cock.

Swords. In some of my former reports I have spoken of the swords furnished by Ames as being of but little account. There are, however, in the hands of some, perhaps a majority, of the men French swords that are in every respect of the first order. They are of the number of the 300 sent out by the Chief of the Ordnance Department to Colonel Kearny some short time since. I wish most sincerely that they may be substituted for our own manufacture throughout.[7]

Saddle and saddle bags. The saddle is without fault, and the saddle bags recently issued are of a more proper size and better shaped than those before inspected by me. Some of the men have still bags of the old pattern.

Jefferson Barracks, August, 1840

The muskets are as clean as it is in the power of the men to keep them, and to judge from their exterior appearance they would be pronounced serviceable, a decision which would not be borne out by the fact. On trial so many of them proved defective that I pronounced them all unserviceable and recommended that they be all turned over to the Ordnance Department and a new issue be made. . . .

Cartridge boxes. Of the latest pattern and decidedly better than any that I have before seen. More pains, however, should be taken with the tin box which contains the cartridge, the edges of which are so rough and sharp that in handling the cartridges the soldier very frequently cuts his hand severely.

Of the bayonet scabbards I have only to say that I have never seen any that even when new were of much account. The belts are good and proper, unless we take into the account the present sword belt of the officer, which, however well it may look on parade, is not suited for the field. I pre-

---

[7] The Ames Sword Company of Chicopee, Massachusetts, was one of the chief American manufacturers of swords for the army. It received its first contract for swords in 1831. For an excellent reference work on the various swords carried by American soldiers, see Harold L. Peterson, *The American Sword, 1775–1945: A Survey of the Swords Worn By the Uniformed Forces of the United States from the Revolution to the Close of World War II* (New Hope, Pennsylvania, 1954).

dict that before the close of the coming year the voice of
every officer will be against their further use.

Fort Atkinson, September 7, 1843

The Dragoon company is better equipped than the companies of the regiment at Fort Leavenworth. The arms, that
is, the carbines and sabres, are the same, and there is little
difference in the cartridge box, but there is an uniformity in
the horse furniture and equipments which gives a finer effect
than was witnessed at the inspection of those companies.
Valises (the first that I have seen) form a part of the equipment, but they are carried only in dress parades and about
the garrison. When on the prairies or upon distant service of
any kind, saddle bags are used, not that objections are urged
against the valise, but because the saddle bags, being more
capacious, enable the men to take with them, besides their
clothing, tobacco and other little things which they deem
essential to comfort on a long march.

Fort Washita, June 19, 1844

The company of the 1st is well mounted, and but that it
has no saddle bags, might take the field at a moment's warn-
ing. The arms (swords excepted) and equipments are old
and in many cases unserviceable or nearly so, but a new
supply will be received very soon, when an exchange will
be made and the old turned in. The companies of the 2nd are
still dismounted, and their entire equipment (that is, their
carbines and cartridge boxes) is worse than I have ever before seen in the course of my military life. I trust that not
many months will elapse before they are well mounted and
fully armed and equipped, that they may assume at least a

respectable standing among these frontier Indians, who if so disposed could cut them off at any moment.

SUTLERS

The army furnished the soldiers with the basic necessities of life—the food, clothing, and equipment with which to carry out their assigned duties. But these were hardly enough to add much pleasure to the life of the man in the ranks. To supply the extras—from tobacco to stationery—each post had a sutler, a civilian attached to the army who ran a general store on the post and who was the old equivalent to the modern post exchange.

"The comfort or well-being of the troops, particularly of those at remote stations, require[s] that the business of sutling should receive a character of permanency, fairness, and respectability"—so read the *Regulations* of 1825. To achieve these ends, detailed regulations were drawn up. There was to be only one sutler to a post, who was formally appointed by the Secretary of War. He was to be assessed a fixed rate (not to exceed 15 cents) per month for every officer and enlisted man at the post, but this was to be the only charge for his monopoly. A council of administration, composed of the senior officers of the post, prescribed the stores which the sutler was to keep and fixed the prices he could charge. In return the sutler was allowed to be present at the pay table in order to collect debts from the soldiers.

The money collected from the sutler by way of assessment formed a post fund, to be used for a variety of good works, including the relief of widows and orphans, the relief of "deranged or decayed officers or infirm or disabled soldiers," education of soldiers' children at a post school, purchase of books for a library, and maintenance of a post band. The sutler was thus an integral part of the garrison, and his store and operations fell under the observation of the Inspector General.[8]

[8] Article 40, *General Regulations for the Army*, 1825.

Fort Mackinac, July 14, 1826

Sutler's store—poorly provided, the requisition made by the board of administration not being yet filled, nor can the deputy left in charge give any satisfactory information as to the probable time of receipt of a sufficient supply.

Fort Atkinson, October, 1826

Sutler—his supply is large, invoiced at $20,000.00. His conduct such as to give satisfaction to the officer in command and to the garrison generally. The council of administration in fixing its prices differs from the mode pursued by other boards. This allows a certain per cent upon the invoice, leaving it with the sutler to distribute such per cent as he may think proper. Other boards place a fixed price upon each individual article. If either mode be defective, it must remain so until altered by the boards themselves, for they recognize no controlling power. I can not in so fit a place suggest the necessity of a general order requiring that once at least in every six months officers at posts shall exhibit to the Pay Master a receipt in full from the sutler, or if this meet not your approbation, that every officer before leaving a post be compelled to pay off his accounts with the sutler. The benefit of the sutler is not here the object so much as the good of the officer. At many of the posts the officers, particularly the younger ones, are greatly in debt, far beyond all immediate hopes of payment, at least from what they receive of the government—and why? The sutler, feeling that he is at the mercy of the officers (for any of them may become members of a board of administration), dare not refuse credit, and the officer, finding his credit good and no pressing calls for money, heedlessly runs into debt and most generally either for borrowed money or for the purchase of those articles which neither he wants nor his more grave wishes could call for. Previous reports to you have recited doubtless more than one instance of the melancholy effects of this unlimited credit.

Fort Jesup, July, 1827

Sutler. Satisfaction is afforded by him to the commanding officer and board of administration. Articles from his store are vended at Natchitoches retail price, cost of carriage from that place superadded. This appears reasonable enough, but withal the soldier pays dearly enough for what he purchases, as the Natchitoches dealers put pretty heavy advances on the New Orleans prices.

Fort Leavenworth, August 26, 1836

The present system of sutling was originated shortly after the war with Great Britain for the twofold purpose of furnishing the soldier with such necessaries as he might want at the cheapest rate and of providing situations of some profit for the support of many of the needy disbanded officers (and so it was understood by both officers and men), but seeing as I do that the good originally intended to be done has been lost sight of, in the latter particular at least, and that sutlers are now appointed from the number of those whom the army know not, I could almost recommend that the whole system be done away with and that we return to things as they were prior to the war.

Fort Crawford, October 11, 1836

Sutlers. Moore and Hallam. These gentlemen have a large assortment of merchandise on hand, many articles of which they vend to the soldiers at a very moderate advance upon their cost, the council of administration having fixed the prices

105

much below the rates in the village of Prairie du Chien. So long as the sutling was confined to disbanded officers, neither officer nor soldier cared how liberal a per centum might be allowed by the council of administration, but now the case is altered. They will not grant a large advance to those with whom they have but little community of feeling.

Fort Winnebago, July 5, 1842

Mr. Clark has not a good supply in store; in truth there is almost a total want of what are called soldier's necessaries. This has been occasioned by the bad appointment made by the council of administration of a sutler prior to the arrival of Captain [William R.] Jouett. The person appointed, having neither money nor credit, could not fulfill his engagements, and thus the recent appointment of Mr. Clark, who will doubtless have in a short time every article that may be wanted.

Fort Brady, September 29, 1843

It appears that the appointment or rather nomination of Mr. Schoolcraft as sutler to the post, although made by a regularly organized council of administration, has not been confirmed by the Secretary of War; this I regret as Mr. Schoolcraft has a large stock of goods on hand which may be sacrificed should another take his place.

I must confess that until this instance I did believe that the nomination of sutler by a council of administration was final, virtually an appointment, and that the *appointment* by the Secretary of War was intended merely to prevent removal by any future council.

5: THE MEN

O F ALL the elements which go to make up an army, the soldiers themselves are by far the most important. Croghan did not neglect them when he came to write his reports. His own sensitive character made him especially alert to their needs and training; his military-mindedness made him picture them in the light of the army as a whole. The result is a series of able comments about the state of discipline and instruction of the soldiers.

DISCIPLINE

One term which seems by nature to go with the word *military* is *discipline*. The essence of a good army turns out to be a fine condition of discipline, of prompt and cheerful adherence to regulations and the commands of superiors on the part of the unit's members. Croghan certainly had this constantly in mind as he made his annual inspections of the western posts. He notes the general disposition of the troops, the numbers in confinement for misbehavior, and the various means adopted by the post commandants to achieve the balance between restriction and freedom upon which good morale depended.

Occasionally, when the opportunity presented itself, Croghan expatiated at length on disciplinary problems. One such problem was corporal punishment (in the form of stripes or lashes), which from time immemorial had been a part of military punishment but which Congress had prohibited in 1812. Another

107

was the curse of desertion, which seriously undermined the very existence of the army. A third concerned the greatest of all banes to proper discipline—too much liquor. Croghan's own difficulties along this line did not blind him to its evils.

There was one song which Croghan sang over and over again. Do not punish the many good soldiers, he insisted, because of a few bad ones. And he repeatedly decried the severe limitations placed on the freedom of the soldiers by post commanders who could think of no other remedy for the drunkenness of their commands. The Inspector General's refrain must have grown monotonous to his superiors, but if there was anything which grieved his heart, it was what he called the "penitentiary" system of discipline. Croghan's feeling for justice and his inherent warmth of character appear nowhere so strongly as in these sections of his reports.

Fort Brady, July 9, 1826

Discipline—good to all appearance and if so in reality not only are the officers deserving of particular credit, but those they command are of better materials than usually fill the ranks of an army. I would with becoming deference note, should the officer in command of this post be a little lax in discipline, ought he to be held to strict account when it is considered how weak are the correctives left in his hands? The 66th Article of War holds out positive encouragement to the soldier to avoid (under certain circumstances) any duty that may be disagreeable to him, and he, aware of this fact, too often commits some trivial offence for the very purpose of being placed in confinement.[1] The warm fireside

[1] Article 66 of the Rules and Articles of War read: "Every officer commanding a regiment or corps, may appoint, for his own regiment or corps, courts martial, to consist of three commissioned officers, for the trial and punishment of offenses, not capital, and decide upon their sentences. For the same purpose, all officers commanding any of the garrisons, forts, bar-

of a guard room is to him rather pleasant when placed in contrast with a hard day's work in the snow or to the handling of a pick axe or spade for half a dozen hours together, at any season. As things now are under the operation of the 66th Article, discipline is preserved, or rather service obtained, not by coercion but by ruinous forbearance. The officer has to coax, he dare not threaten; he is in the power of the soldier who exerts it whenever he is not treated with *reverence* due his *rank* and *high station*. For offences not capital, the person in the permanent command of a post, be he but a sergeant, should have the right to order courts martial and to pass upon their decisions. Punishments to have their due effect should follow immediately on the heels of the offences. It has more than once occurred that a soldier has been in voluntary confinement here for months before a court could be ordered for his trial, and even after being arraigned before the court as many months more elapse before its sentence was officially announced.

Fort Armstrong, August, 1826
Discipline. Everything bespeaks its correctness. At no post which I have visited have I remarked more perfect order or more ready and apparently cheerful obedience. This is the second day of my sojourn, and during this time nothing that could either offend the eye or the ear has been noticed. At the usual hour of retiring at night all became as still and hushed as if there had been but one family. I do not disparage

racks, or other places, where the troops consist of different corps, may assemble courts martial, to consist of three commissioned officers, and decide upon their sentences." This provision did not permit the commandants of most small western posts to institute a court martial. Thus, immediate punishment was not possible, and a culprit might be confined for a long period before a court martial could be arranged.

Major [Josiah H.] Vose's merits as a disciplinarian in questioning if all this be not ascribable in a great measure to the almost entire expulsion of whiskey from the garrison. No soldier can obtain permission to purchase of the sutler more than one gill at a time, and that must be drunk at his counter. The ration itself is dealt out at two different periods. Half a gill just before breakfast, the remaining half at dinner, both at the mess room door.[2]

Fort St. Philip, June, 1827

The quarters now erecting and nearly completed are airy, roomy, and may be found convenient, but the location of that portion of them designed for the officers is odd enough, being 100 yards without the work and for aught I know, more. He who made this disposition must have had some particularly select company under view for the garrison; of the non-commissioned officers and soldiers that are commonly met with in our ranks, but a very few are sufficiently trustworthy to be left even for a single night in charge of a fortress, particularly of one so important as this.

Fort Jesup, July, 1827

Discipline—very perfect and I am pleased that I can say it is preserved without any apparent exertion. I have no where witnessed more harmony and good feeling than prevails here.

[2] The daily ration, established in 1802, allowed for a gill of rum, whiskey, or brandy. In 1830 ardent spirits ceased to be issued because "the habitual use of ardent spirits by the troops, has a pernicious effect upon their health, morals, and discipline." A sum of money was at first allowed in lieu of the whiskey ration, but in 1832 the commutation in money was stopped and an issue of sugar and coffee substituted. Order No. 72, Adjutant General's Office, December 8, 1830, and Order No. 100, Headquarters of the Army, Adjutant General's Office, November 5, 1832. The soldiers, however, managed to get a copious supply of liquor from other sources.

Every officer appears anxious to forward the wishes of his brother officer, and the men, although not hemmed in by sentinels and left free to roam where they will, seldom abuse the confidence reposed in them. To what is this happy state of things to be ascribed? To the prompt and equally certain infliction of punishment consequent upon the commission of an offence which prevails here, or to that just administration of police which, by allowing every reasonable indulgence to the correct soldier, seems coercive only when applied to such as have already forfeited all claims to confidence; or is it to both conjointly? I speak of the facts as they exist; the cause inducing is left for others to determine.

Jefferson Barracks, November 10, 1833

The order prohibiting the sale of whiskey or other spirituous liquor by the sutler has not been attended by the happy results expected from it.[3] On the contrary, it has at some of the posts (let me instance Forts Howard and Crawford and Jefferson Barracks) rather added to than lessened the vice of intemperance, in a word, has virtually given us, instead of sutlers observant of regulations and obedient to orders, numerous retailers of spirits who, regardless of the consequences to the soldiers, vie with each other in their efforts to wheedle them from their quarters at all hours of the night to join in scenes of drunkenness and riot. Withdraw then the prohibition upon the sutlers; let the councils of administration reduce the price of their liquors so as barely to cover expences, and a corrective to all this is at once found; the retailers who infest the garrisons will at once retire (as they

[3] The prohibition, issued first in 1830 and 1832, appeared in Paragraph 19, Article 32 of the 1835 edition of *General Regulations for the Army:* "Sutlers are not to keep ardent spirits, nor are they to mix them with any beverage allowed to be sold to the troops, under the penalty of losing their situations."

can not live by honest and reasonable profits), and the soldiers will no longer be induced to wander abroad to procure that which they can obtain of the sutler so long as he sees that they indulge not too freely. Debar by order a soldier from the use of spirituous liquor and you at once create in him an appetite for it; you induce him to get drunk who was never known to indulge too freely when he was left at liberty to drink whenever he thought proper.

Washington, December 9, 1833

Query 4th.[4] "On the effect produced on the discipline of the army by the abolishing of stripes or lashes in all cases save those of desertion."[5]

Of myself I can say nothing positive on this subject as my recent experience is but trifling, but if the opinion of a majority of the most intelligent gentlemen of the army be received by you, I must declare it to be in favor of corporal punishments by stripes or lashes as necessary to the preservation of more perfect discipline. Occasionally I have met with officers of equal intelligence who thought differently, but they were of less practical experience, perhaps, and of the number of those who view the materials which fill the ranks of our army as composed of men such as they should be, not as they really are. Were every soldier a proud, high minded citizen, we would all at once declare our perfect indifference about the modes of punishment or indeed whether or not any at all were allowed, but as this is very far from

---

[4] For Croghan's answer to another query in this series, see pages 12–24.

[5] Congress in 1812 prohibited the use of whipping as a military punishment. The prohibition was generally considered detrimental to good discipline by military commanders, and in 1833 the punishment of whipping was restored for men convicted by a general court martial of the crime of desertion. *United States Statutes at Large,* II, 735; IV, 647.

being the case, and that too many are of a description of persons dead to everything like moral feelings and whom nothing can degrade or humiliate, we ought not to withhold from our courts martial the power to inflict upon such subjects either stripes or lashes or such other substituted punishments as may be *brief* and thus be the most likely to coerce them to a proper performance of their duties, with the least possible inconvenience to the good and correct soldier, whose duties under existing circumstances multiply exactly in proportion to the bad subjects in his particular company.

Should a board for the revision of the rules and articles of war be at any time ordered to convene, no question could with more propriety be submitted to it than the one now under consideration, for its decision in relation thereto would be presumed upon the practical experience of years and divested of those speculative notions that have led many into the error of believing that our soldiers are without an exception possessed of a higher grade of mental delicacy than those of any other power upon earth and that they should therefore never be mortified by a suggestion even that the mode of punishment by stripes or lashes now in vogue in other services might ere long be renewed here.

Had some of our legislators a little more practical experience on the subject, they would not fear the results that they now apprehend; it would be evident to them that we have some soldiers in our ranks who do not look upon stripes as at all more degrading than any other mode of punishment, and that the good and correct soldier would freely advocate the restitution of the lash, as perhaps the only mode whereby such vile offenders might be coerced to bear at least some little share of duty. I am disposed to believe from much personal enquiry on the subject that a majority of our rank and file do not at all thank those who have so kindly volunteered their sympathies, for they can not be induced to believe that they will be degraded and ill used whenever our courts martial are again vested with power to sentence to stripes. They have too much confidence in the integrity and correct feeling of their officers to apprehend anything for themselves, and they are of course not disposed to spare any longer those worthless fellows for whom they have from the first been compelled to do an extra share of duty. And why should the correct soldier care about the severity of the punishment attendant upon crimes, any more than any gentleman of the country should feel uneasy at the thought that in his particular state branding was the punishment for hog stealing.

Query 5. Desertions. To what causes are they attributable?[6]

The causes which induce discontent and consequent desertion are doubtless pretty much the same at all our posts, but what those causes really are is as yet but a matter of conjecture. From frequent conversations on the subject with officers and intelligent non-commissioned officers at different times and places, it would seem that some of the sources of discontent are derived from the following causes, viz.—

1st. The mode of making the payments.

[6] The rate of desertion in the army was extremely high. In 1823 desertions equaled one-fourth of the enlistments in that year and in 1826 more than half. Of 5,000 men in the army in 1830, 1,200 deserted. Secretary of War Jefferson Davis reported in 1853 that the average annual loss by desertion between 1826 and 1845 had been 12¾ per cent and that after the Mexican War it climbed to 16 per cent. Reports of Adjutant General Roger Jones, January 11, 1826, and December 31, 1827, in *American State Papers: Military Affairs*, III, 228, 689; Report of the Secretary of War, 1831, *ibid.*, IV, 708; Report of the Secretary of War, 1853, in 33 Cong., 1 sess., *Senate Executive Doc. No. 1*, part 2, pp. 7–8 (serial 691). For further statistics see *American State Papers: Military Affairs*, III, 194–99, 274–77.

2nd. The want of authority to institute courts for the summary infliction of punishments for offences.

3rd. The want of uniformity in the articles of company police in the different companies belonging to the same garrison or detachment.

4th. The uncertainty of punishments and their extreme diversity when inflicted.

First. The mode of making payments. Payments should be made more frequently, once a week or at most once a fortnight. Soldiers are most commonly but bad accountants and thus when called at the end of several months to the pay table, instead of having to pocket a few dollars with which to pay off their little debts to their citizen acquaintances of the neighbourhood (and about which alone they feel solicitude), they see the whole amount due to them by the government swept off by the sutler for they know not what, or rather for the payment of articles purchased some time before though now forgotten. Disappointment and chagrin are the consequences, and they retire to their quarters, there to brood over their discontent, not with a determination to economize for the future, but to give vent to their dislike to a service which affords them neither peace within nor without the camp and to concert among themselves upon the speediest and safest mode of getting rid of it. A soldier wishes money, not so much that he has necessary wants to provide for, but that he has a desire to spend it among his citizen associates, for seeing that his consequence among them rests mainly upon his ability to spend that which they have not, so his contentedness with the service is exactly in proportion to the opportunities which it affords him for shewing off this consequence.

Payment every week, with a positive injunction upon the

sutler on no account to grant credits, would in all save the most inveterate cases produce this desired end, for by thus enabling the soldier at all times to know the exact state of his account, he will be guarded against contracting debts, especially to citizens, which if long unpaid will cause him more annoyance than the severest duties of his garrison. He becomes a prisoner in his own camp and can not venture out of it even to recreate himself for fear of meeting the scoffs and jeerings of his former associates and creditors. Some will have it that not only is the present term of payment full often enough, but that even one half of the pay should be retained until the expiration of the enlistment as a pledge for the services of the soldier.

How far the adoption of such a rule would operate as a preventive against desertion will be presently seen from the following fact which occurred on my last visit to Hancock Barracks. The opinion of an intelligent sergeant having been asked as to the effect that would probably be produced by the retention of one half the pay as above stated, [he] answered, "It would dissatisfy the correct soldiers, and the worthless who might be tempted to desert would not be kept back by the assurance that even *$200* would be paid to them on the expiration of their terms of enlistment; so little do they care about money not already in hand that they will barter their pay for a month for a mere trifle. I can," continued he, "purchase tea in this village at 40 cents a pound that has just cost at the sutler's store $1.50. The tea having in the first instance been procured from the sutler by soldiers under stoppage of their whiskey, by them exchanged with citizens for ardent spirits, and by them in turn sold at a heavy advance at the low price stated." Need anything more be said against an adoption of the opinion that much good would be found to derive from a retention of the monthly pay?

Second. The want of authority to institute garrison courts for the summary infliction of punishment for offences.

Unless punishments follow immediately upon the heels of offences, discipline can not be properly enforced, and what officer is there who has not experienced the truth of this remark and deplored the very limited powers entrusted to commandants of posts in relation to courts martial? In truth, the evils growing out of this inability to order courts are almost without number, and they tend more than any other circumstances to weary and distress commandants of posts and companies and to dissatisfy the soldiery. Worthless soldiers use it as a screen to protect themselves from all unpleasant tours of service, and they find it a most complete one. If the service is to be unpleasant, they decide in favor of the guard house during its continuance and commit some offence for the very purpose of being placed in confinement, well knowing that on affecting penitence with a promise of behaving better for the future, they will be at once released (to play the same game over again) rather than be kept for months awaiting a court martial.

Worthy soldiers are oppressed by it, for in proportion to the number of scoundrels screened is the increased amount of duty imposed upon them. They consequently become sooner or later dissatisfied with a service in which the offending and worthless go unpunished, and the worthy alone are pressed upon. Officers, in the warmth of their zeal to correct the flagrant abuses which they find to exist and to equalize duty as far as practicable, sometimes forget themselves and take the law into their own hands, thus jeoparding their commissions in the vain effort to compel those worthless drones of the army to take upon themselves the extra share of duty which they impose upon more worthy members. Non-commissioned officers, too, from the same cause become discontented. Held to strict account and perhaps at times spoken roughly to by their officers for permitting disorderly conduct in their squads or for some other supposed acts of willful negligence, they in a moment of irritation deal in violent language and perhaps blows among the offending, in this way forfeiting their rank and furnishing to those whom they have punished the convenient and common excuse for desertion, "ill usage and abuse from the non-commissioned officers." Punish a soldier legally for the commission of an offence and he will forgive you because it is the law not you, but resort to the only coercive weapons now left unfortunately, and you drive him from the service.

Third. The want of uniformity in the articles of company police.

I assume as a fact that there are fewer desertions in proportion to numerical strength from those posts garrisoned by a single company than will be found to take place from those composed of two or more. In garrisons consisting of several companies each captain or officer in command of a company establishes of himself his own system of rules for the internal government of his company (and from the nature of his responsibilities it could not well be otherwise). These rules are consequently as diverse as the dispositions and temperament of the persons originating them, and to this diversity must be ascribed a good deal of the grumbling and discontent that we find at times to exist. The soldiers of one company will be found at liberty to go where they please and do as they like during the intervals of duty, whilst those of

118

another are kept within the sentinels and not permitted to go beyond them without a written pass and then but seldom. What must follow? Dissatisfaction of course. Why, say the restricted soldiers, this unequal distribution of favors? What have we done that we are thus unjustly deprived of privileges which are so freely awarded to others placed by the law upon the same footing with ourselves? We have complained, but only to make matters worse. We will now take advantage of the first opportunity which is afforded for escape to desert a service in which we have suffered nothing but ill usage.

Soldiers are exactly like individuals in other communities, a little jealous. They will patiently bear, and without feeling it burthensome, all that the most rigid rules of police demand, but no sooner do they discover that they alone are required to conform to them, whilst others are allowed greater licence, then all is seen through a different medium. That which before was mere wholesome discipline has now become oppression and tyranny.

A partial corrective to this is at all times in the hands of commandants of posts. They can not or ought not, it is true, to assume the internal government of each company, but it is their duty at all events to take care that all soldiers of their respective commands be alike allowed every liberty not prohibited by special garrison regulations (unless good cause for restriction be made in every case fully to appear) and that no duties be required of them other than those clearly implied by the nature of their engagement with the government and as far as practicable exclusively on public account.

Fourth. The uncertainty of punishments and their extreme diversity.

The uncertainty of punishment arises out of the difficulty of obtaining courts martial, and thus the impunity with which trivial offences may be committed leads step by step to those of a more serious character, and in the end to mutiny, murder, or desertion, and the diversity in the modes of punishment is to be ascribed to the too great latitude left with our courts in determining crime and affixing its penalty, and hence it is that upon our records there may be found stated a greater variety of punishments for the same offence than there are definable offences. Dissatisfaction must grow out of such a state of things, and if as I remarked just now, discontent is occasioned by a mere difference in company administration, how much more must take place when for the commission of the same offence courts shall be found to award to some prisoners a very severe sentence and to others one amounting to almost an acquittal.

Let the law then declare what shall constitute crime and affix thereto appropriate punishments, so as to leave nothing for the courts but to determine upon the guilt or innocence of those arraigned, for until then will the causes of dissatisfaction as above stated continue to exist.

But be the causes which lead to desertion as they may, the frequency of the crime would doubtless be greatly lessened by the establishment by law of a mode of punishment which should visit with *certainty* and equally upon all offenders without regard to persons or to mitigating circumstances. The *certainty* rather than the *severity* of punishments operates as a preventive to crime, and thus with desertion. Let the sentence of every offender on apprehension and conviction be as follows, to receive the full number of lashes allowed by law, to work in chains upon the fortresses or other public works until the close of his enlistment, and then to be branded upon the shoulder in such a manner as to preclude the possibility of his ever again enlisting as a soldier or of obtaining

120

service of any kind from the government. An objection may be urged against the mode of punishment here suggested, upon the ground that it visits with equal severity upon all offenders. To it I answer, that as for the future I would have no *second* desertions. I have but classed every case that may occur as of the same rank in point of enormity because they must all be of *first* occurrence.

Fort Winnebago, August 7, 1834
I regret to state that 16 privates are in confinement, most of them for drunkenness, which can not be prevented by the utmost vigilance of the officers of the post. The soldier disposed to drink has only to elude the sentinels and he can obtain liquor to any amount at a shop a mile and a half off on the bank of the Ouisconsin, belonging to a man who can not be reached by any military process.

Fort Snelling, October 7, 1836
At no post visited by me have I witnessed more order or more cheerfulness and apparent content among the soldiery. The discipline is of course good and exact. Much praise is due to Lieutenant Colonel [William] Davenport for this state of things, but something too must be credited to the fact that no whiskey can be brought into this part of the country to make the soldier forget that exact obedience is at all times expected of him.

Fort Crawford, October 11, 1836
I believe that the utmost pains are taken by the officers present to carry into effect the wholesome regulations of the post, but surrounded as the place is by dram shops, which are at all hours open to the soldiers, the task is attended with

more of care and watchfulness than of success. This I have learned from the officers themselves and not from personal observations, for as yet nothing has met my eye which would indicate a want of order or the most exact subordination.

Service. The details are made with as due regard to an equal apportionment as practicable, but they nevertheless fall most heavily upon the good and correct soldiers, who have not only to perform their own proper share of duty, but also that of every skulking subject of the guard house. And this is the case at every other post, as the number of the worthless, so in like proportion do the duties devolve upon the worthy and industrious soldiers. Restore the lash, give to commandants of posts authority to institute garrison courts martial, and this evil would be corrected in a great degree, for then there would be no sending to the guard house unless for capital offences, but punishments would follow immediately upon the heels of offences, and those committing them, at once turned over to their companies for duty.

Fort Crawford, September, 1840

Discipline. Sufficiently rigid. General [George M.] Brooke's system of police of garrison government is illy calculated to attain for him the objects he so studiously aims at, the reclamation of the dissipated and worthless soldier and the non-contamination of the good and exemplary, for it would seem to make no other distinction between the bad and good than this—that the first have committed outrages and the latter would do so likewise had they the free liberty of action. No non-commissioned officer or soldier is permitted to leave the fort even for an instant without a pass signed by his company officer and countersigned by the commandant of the place. This is all wrong. Confine as much as you choose the soldier who misbehaves, but grant every reasonable indulgence to such as have never abused your confidence. The correct and faithful soldier becomes dissatisfied, and in the end negligent in the performance of his duties at being thus confined and trammeled during the intervals of duty (hours which he may have been accustomed to consider as his own), and the worthless one, seeing that even the most exemplary behaviour is met by no commensurate benefits, feels no promptings or incentives to a change of habit. I have thus spoken of General Brooke's system of police as too exact and indiscriminating, but it is not here only that a similar one is in full exercise. Too many other commandants of posts thus punish the many worthy for the faults of the few undeserving, to the injury of both.

Detroit, June 16, 1842

Here, as at most if not all of our military posts, discipline is sought to be obtained by a system of coercion or strictness of police at variance at least with my former practice and present opinions, which would lead me to operate upon the soldier by appealing to his pride and finer feelings rather than to his baser passion, fear. Let me not be understood as charging want of discipline upon this command, but only as protesting against the course pursued towards its attainment. I would have the soldier treated as a *man* and entitled to confidence until he shall prove himself unworthy of it and not as a *fellow* to be watched, as though he would do right only under compulsion. At every post in the country in a greater or less degree the many are punished for the faults of the few. For what is it but a punishment to confine soldiers to their quarters at all times unless when permitted occasionally to leave them under a written pass. They ought to be permitted to go where they please within the radius of a mile when not on duty, and to debar them from so doing unless under particular circumstances ought to be viewed as a breach of their privileges. Custom has sanctioned the present system, but the Articles of War do not seem to warrant it. See Articles 41 to 44, inclusive.[7] But let the law be as it may, I am persuaded that the most fruitful source of discontent among our troops (and thus the cause of most of the desertions) is to be found in the practice of which I complain and which I trust may ere long be discontinued.

There are here, out of force of 245 non-commissioned officers and privates (15 having been deducted as sick in hospital), 41 in confinement, most of them for drunkenness; what a commentary upon the present system of restraints! Could there have been a greater number in confinement, could there have been even so many, had the gates been thrown wide open for all to pass out at will.

Fort Crawford, July 11, 1842

Colonel [William] Davenport in all that he does acts with strict impartiality and with an eye single to the public service, but the whole of his system of police by which he would encourage and maintain proper discipline is most obviously ill judged and wrong. As General Brooke's course in relation to the enforcement of discipline was declared to be unwise

[7] "Article 41. All non-commissioned officers and soldiers who shall be found one mile from the camp, without leave in writing, from their commanding officer, shall suffer such punishment as shall be inflicted upon them by the sentence of a court martial.

"Article 42. No officer or soldier shall lie out of his quarters, garrison, or camp, without leave from his superior officer, upon penalty of being punished according to the nature of his offence, by the sentence of a court martial.

"Article 43. Every non-commissioned officer and soldier shall retire to his quarters or tent, at the beating of the retreat; in default of which he shall be punished according to the nature of his offence."

if not unauthorized by law in my report from Detroit, so in like manner I must declare against the system pursued by Colonel Davenport as certainly calculated to produce dissatisfaction and consequent desertion, and in the end effect the destruction of his command.

A standing garrison order permits four men only (taken in rotation from each company) per day to leave the fort. Thus even the very best soldiers are restricted to one, at most two, indulgences in a month. Can anything be more oppressive or more obviously wrong? I have spoken much to the Colonel, but he will not be persuaded or turned from his course. He insists, as did General Brooke, that were he to relax, duty could not be done, so many would be the drunken. In this he is surely mistaken, and were he at once to throw wide open his gates, a week would not pass before he would become convinced that he had been persisting in an unfortunate error. That there are confirmed drunkards in his command I have not a doubt, but they were such before enlistment. If any have become so since, it may be charged mainly to his ill-judged severity. During the 17 years of my official intercourse as Inspector General with the army I have remarked drunkenness to prevail directly in proportion to the restraints imposed upon the liberty of the soldier.

If you would guard against the enlistment of confirmed drunkards and of persons labouring under chronic diseases, assign an army surgeon or assistant to our principal recruiting stations. Citizen surgeons are not to be relied on; they too often pass men that a more scrutinizing eye would at once detect and reject. If you desire to lessen the amount of drunkenness now prevailing, rescind the order prohibiting the sale of spirituous liquors by the sutler (for commandants of posts are doubtful of their authority on the subject), and you at once strike at the root of the evil, you put to flight the scores of whiskey dealers that infest our posts, vying with each other in efforts to entice the soldier away from his duty to join them in scenes of drunkenness and riot.

It is well that whiskey as part of the ration has been discontinued; it doubtless caused many to drink the allowance rather than throw it away. It was esteemed as almost essential to the character of the recruit that he should be able to take his portion, and thus the habit of drinking became in a manner confirmed—but such would not be the case were permission granted to purchase at will of the sutler, he being held responsible that no improper indulgences were permitted.

Fort Snelling, July 16, 1842

Unlike the state of things at Fort Crawford, here every soldier is allowed to pass out at will during the day unless his conduct has been such as to render him unworthy of such indulgence, and as might be expected, there are comparatively but few abuses committed. There are not as many whiskey shops in the immediate vicinity as there are about Fort Crawford, but still there is at all times whiskey enough to supply those who have money to pay for it. The last steam boat brought up 20 barrels, which were landed below the military reserve on the east bank of the river, all doubtless for retail to the soldiery, who indulge as often as they may feel disposed, provided their cash be not expended, and just in like manner would they indulge were they confined within the walls of the fort. Wherever there is money with persons disposed to drink there will be no lack of whiskey.

Steamer Ohio, *August 27, 1843*

I can not do justice to the feelings of satisfaction which I

126

experienced during my recent visit of inspection to Jefferson Barracks, for rarely if ever during my long intercourse with the army have I witnessed so happy a state of things, so pleasing a picture of garrison life. In all that large society there seemed not one discordant element, every thing moved on harmoniously, and the daily routine of duty appeared no longer monotonous, being worked into life and spirit by the generous emulation of the two corps composing the garrison.

Jefferson Barracks, August, 1843

Correct discipline must be maintained, else I had not witnessed such a state of things as was spoken of at the commencement of this report. The large number in confinement (102) would seem to argue much against the proper temper of the rank and file of the brigade, but it must be borne in mind that very many of the confined are lovers of strong drink, who have made themselves amenable to a court martial through their irresistible appetite for the bottle, rather than from any mutinous spirit or rooted feeling of opposition to the established rules of order and proper government. There are here though, as well as at other posts, discontented soldiers, restless mutinous fellows, who take pleasure in trying the temper and patience of the officer to the very utmost, and this class is rather on the increase and from a cause which will I trust ere long manifest itself to you.

Fort Atkinson, September 7, 1843

A great change has been wrought in the appearance of things since July, 1842. Then there [were] discontent and frequent desertions among the soldiery, the work itself was unfinished and went on slowly from the want of funds, which it was apprehended might be withheld altogether. Now content and order are depicted upon every countenance, the whole establishment is completed, and everything within and without tells of a well-established fort, regularly garrisoned and with regular troops. The garrison consists of two companies and 97 rank and file, commanded by Captain [Edwin V.] Sumner of the Dragoons.

Fort Crawford, September 11, 1843

It would seem that a wholesome and proper discipline prevailed, and that too without coercion, so marked seem the order and content on every hand, and yet this is not to be accounted for without ascribing something personal to the present commandant, for his garrison rules are little less restrictive than those of his predecessor, about which I complained so much in my last report. The number of desertions and confinements in the guard house during the quarters ending in July, 1842 and 1843, was about the same, reference being had to the strength of the companies at those two periods, but trials by courts martial were fewer by one half in 1843 than in the corresponding quarter of 1842, a fact in itself quite insufficient to account for the change that has to all appearance been effected. I would not be understood as approving *in extenso* the system of Lieutenant Colonel [Henry] Wilson, which is too exacting and restrictive, although less so than that of his predecessor, Colonel Davenport. I still insist than an officer has no right to confine an unoffending soldier to his barrack yard during the intervals of duty, and further that drunkenness and other offences prevail directly in proportion to the restraints imposed on the liberty of the soldier. An officer in striking a soldier under whatever provocation jeopards his commission, and yet he is permitted to confine him for months to the narrow limits of his barrack, be his conduct as exemplary as it may—an exercise of official tyranny unknown, at all events unauthorized, I venture to affirm, in either the French or English service. I sincerely trust that sooner or later this subject may be brought up for consideration, as until it shall be and proper correction applied, the good soldier will have to bear many unnecessary crosses.

Plattsburgh Barracks, November 8, 1843

I have now completed my inspection of the Dragoons and the five Infantry regiments stationed on the Missouri and Mississippi rivers and the lakes, but before closing this dispatch, I would express to you the gratification which I have experienced in witnessing the very great improvement which has been made within the last 18 months in every regiment or command visited by me. That some are more advanced than others may not be denied, but as the difference is not very wide and that all are striving for mastery with a most generous emulation, it may be safely inferred that in the course of another year all will be so nearly alike as to exhibit no points of dissimilitude. But it is not alone in the knowledge of his various duties that the soldier has advanced; his moral condition is likewise much better and is brought under a discipline such as I have not before seen since 1826–27. I speak generally, for there are instances doubtless at variance with this declaration.

It may be said that most of the worthless and abandoned men having been got rid of, either by expiration of enlistment or sentence of a court martial, the happy change that has taken place might have been expected. Be it so, we have it proven to us at all events that the enlistment of men insensible to moral restraints adds nothing to the effective strength of

129

our regiments. Captain [Carlos A.] Waite says of his fine company that there are four or five men whom no course of treatment can recover or correct and who, so far from bearing their proper share of duty, are as . . . a dead weight upon the rest of the command, and so it ever is. The severity of duty in a company is directly as the number of worthless subjects in that company.

Such men are not worth the cost of a court martial; why not then discharge them upon the certificate of their captain approved by the colonel of the regiment. By so doing, our effective strength would be much increased and the character of the army elevated. No danger could result from the adoption of such a course. We should only part with the worthless, for no captain of the army would ask the discharge of a man out of whom he might in the end make a good soldier.

Baton Rouge, May 8, 1844

Discipline. At present good and correct. A great change for the better has been wrought in the habits and temper of this command; but a short time ago there was much intemperance with great insubordination. Now a drunken soldier is but seldom seen, and cheerful and ready obedience is given to every order. A post temperance society has been organized, over which one of the non-commissioned officers presides, and already one half of the men have enrolled themselves as members.[8] Here as at New Orleans the soldiers go unques-

[8] Temperance societies among the soldiers were common, although they appear generally to have been shortlived. At Fort Snelling a society reported sixty-eight members, including two officers, in 1836. See the long "Address of the Temperance Society of Fort Snelling," an appeal to the soldiers to adopt a temperance program, in *Army and Navy Chronicle,* Vol. II (1836), 301–303. A temperance society at Fort Howard at one time had eighty members pledged to total abstinence. Jackson Kemper, "Journal of an Episcopalian

tioned during the intervals of duty, and such should be the case at every post in the country.

Fort Jesup, May 14, 1844

I have never before seen so fine a command, and I question whether a better in every respect is to be found anywhere. Discipline the most perfect prevails throughout, and that too, as some will have it, under every discouragement, as all around are lures to draw the soldier away from his duty. There are billiard tables, ninepin alleys, ball alleys, a theatre, and shops kept by citizens at which liquors are sold to all who call for them, be they soldiers or citizens. And whence comes it that amidst all these temptations the soldiers are never for a moment forgetful of themselves or unmindful of the obligations which their enlistment imposes? Why simply from this, they are treated as men in whom confidence may be placed, and they take pride in proving to their officers that they have not overestimated their worth. How have you wrought so happy a change, said I to Colonel [David E.] Twiggs. He answered, by putting an end to the old penitentiary system. And what would be the effect of your return to it—to have ⅓ of my command drunk in a week.

I have said more than once in my reports that the offences committed by the soldier are always directly as the restraints imposed upon him. I trust that you will take this matter into your own hands, that at least the good and correct soldier may no longer suffer from the faults of the undeserving. The penitentiary system ought to be exploded; the many should no longer be punished for the misdeeds of the few. If there be soldiers whom no course of treatment can recover, discharge

Missionary's Tour to Green Bay, 1834," *Wisconsin Historical Collections,* XIV, 415.

them without trial upon the certificate of the company officer and commandant of the regiment. Economy and comfort would be alike promoted by such a course. Bad men may increase your numerical force, but can add nothing to its efficiency; on the contrary lessen it.

Fort Washita, June 19, 1844

In a garrison so constituted or rather so drawn off and separated upon various duties none of them properly appertaining to the soldier and the most of them performed without the presence of an officer, it is impossible to form a positive opinion as to the state of its discipline from actual personal observation. The general reputation of the commandant as a disciplinarian and the appearance and demeanor of the men constitute the best, if not the only true test whereby a judgment may be formed. In the present case, I must declare the discipline to be proper, as after two weeks' sojourn I have remarked nothing indicative of a restless, insubordinate spirit among the soldiery or a disposition on the part of any officer to be either too lax or too exacting. Brevet Major [Benjamin L.] Beall, who was in command until the arrival of Colonel [William S.] Harney a few days ago, has been indebted, I think, mainly to the fine materials of which his command is composed for this happy state of things. I may be mistaken in my estimate of the Major's powers, still I can not but think he would have failed under the circumstances with troops of a different temperament. The officers of this command (unless in a single case, that of Captain [Marshall S.] Howe, whom none speak to unless on duty) harmonize well together, and yet they have an unpleasant time of it, from the very fact that they want occupation. Their men being taken from them to become house builders, etc., they are thus deprived of the stimulation of the drill, always so delightful to the soldier. Colonel Harney avers that he will dispel this tediousness by requiring sabre exercise every morning and evening and readings of the Dragoon and Infantry tactics at stated hours through the day. . . .

Mr. ——— with permission of Colonel Harney is fitting up a house, in which are to be a billiard table, ninepin alleys, and a refreshment room furnished with every variety of liquors, and open to all officers and at stated hours to such soldiers (and to those only) as merit every indulgence. My belief is that much good will be derived from this establishment, particularly in its effects upon the hitherto intemperate, who will strive to merit all the indulgences granted to his more exemplary fellow soldier. At all events such has been the effect produced at Fort Jesup by the licensing of similar establishments.

Watch as you may, the soldier who *will* have whiskey *can* procure it. Put not therefore too many restraints upon the good soldier, but during the intervals of duty let him feel that the time is his own, to pass it as he may in any innocent amusement. Men who have no intellectual enjoyments ought to be encouraged to engage in athletic exercises and not chided as they sometimes are for boisterous mirth, as unbecoming. We can't make saints, but we may have soldiers.

INSTRUCTION AND DUTIES

Unfailingly Croghan reported on two items of garrison activity which bore the technical names *instruction* and *service*. The first is self-explanatory; it dealt with the expertness of the troops in executing the exercises prescribed for their proper arm of the military service. Croghan would draw up the troops to check their efficiency in drill and in the execution of set infantry or light infantry tactics. The second covered the distribution of fatigue duties among the individual members of the command. Under this head the Inspector General commented on the nature, severity, and fairness in the distribution of these duties. The two elements were inversely correlative: where the fatigue duties were heavy, instruction was poor. The men and officers did not have time and energy enough to do both.

There can be no question about Croghan's attitude as to where the proper emphasis should be placed. Soldiers should be soldiers, not workmen. Laments echo through the pages of his reports about the heavy duties required of the men in gathering fuel for the fireplaces or hay for the livestock or about the dismal state of instruction on account of the immense labors required in the building of a new post.

Fort Snelling, August, 1826

Instruction. Not very perfect and yet as good and perhaps better than could or ought to be expected under all circumstances. Look at Fort Snelling as it now stands, be told that it was erected in six years by the soldiers themselves, who at the same time were tillers of the soil to the extent of many hundred acres, and you will feel disposed to give them credit if they have preserved even the proper *feelings* of the *soldier,* instruction in the duties justly appertaining to their situation out of the question. There is much intelligence among the officers of the garrison, and it is to be regretted that circumstances should have rendered it necessary to direct it toward objects so wide of the mark it would wish to have aimed at. "We have lost almost all that we once knew, but as our labours as farmers and builders are now comparatively closed we hope soon to recover our lost ground." Such is the language held by more than one officer of this garrison.

Fort Armstrong, August, 1826

Instruction. Not very good (to Infantry drill I allude), arising from the want of practise on the part of both officers and men. Major [Josiah H.] Vose informs me that one of his officers recently from St. Peters had not taken part in a drill previous to his arrival here during the last four or five years, his time having been doubtless entirely occupied in other duties than those appertaining in however remote a degree to the school of the soldier. The course now pursued will doubtless lead to rapid improvement and before the end of the year to comparative perfection. Two hours in the morning and the like time in the afternoon are devoted to the Infantry drill, the company officers commanding in turn and always under the eye of the commanding officer of the post.

Fort Atkinson, October, 1826

Service. As regular and as equally distributed as the various duties to be performed can admit of. The roster at these frontier posts can not be looked to. The book of general regulations in all that may relate to the distribution of duties had as well be laid upon the shelf.

Fort Gibson, August, 1827

The colonel certainly has the interest of the government exclusively at heart and strives to the utmost to give satisfaction; he thinks that the main object is to keep the soldier constantly on fatigue, and he acts with ready obedience to this supposed wish; and can he think otherwise when he reflects upon the character of service which his regiment has performed since its first coming to the country and of that which it has now to perform. The cutting of three roads is imposed upon it. One from Natchitoches to Cantonment Towson, another from Cantonment Towson to Fort Smith on the Arkansas, and the third from Fort Smith to Cantonment Gibson, in all more than 500 miles.

I have not seen the act of Congress providing for the making of these roads and know nothing about the arguments used in bringing about its passage, but I boldly assert that had the subject been well understood by a majority of the members of Congress, it would not have passed; and that if he who first offered it did understand it, he acted from motives *best known to himself.* I have recently passed over a greater part of the road from Natchitoches to Cantonment Towson and found no interruptions on the way, nor did I hear even from the inhabitants themselves complaints about the badness of the travelling. Carriages pass freely along the whole distance. Why then the necessity for this road? I have just come, too, along the path leading from Cantonment Towson to Fort Smith on the Arkansas. The way is somewhat circuitous, in part mountainous and of difficult passage; it might be better, but what then will be gained? For what description of travellers is the road to be made? For Indians—they never travel a road—for citizens—not a dozen pass in a year, and they, like the Indians, avoid the beaten path for the purpose of killing game. The soldiers—they but seldom pass along, and when they do, they find the path wide enough. They have, besides, a nearer way from Cantonment Towson to Gibson by sixty miles. The road now under view passes through a perfectly desolate country belonging to the Choctaws, all of whom are on the other side of the Red River. The Choctaw agent, his interpreter, and blacksmith, with a few miserable squatters, are its only inhabitants. The road from Fort Smith to this place, recently cut by a detail of two commissioned officers and 50 men from this garrison at a cost of four months' labour, is found on the part first made to be grown up in bushes to the height of four or five feet—a proof of the *great travelling*. The old road is perhaps longer than this by five or six miles, but it is withal so good a way that it continues to be travelled over and has been for years found wide enough for the loads of whiskey which have been smuggled into this neighbourhood for the especial use of the soldiers.

There is intelligence with just pride among the officers of the army, and they desire nothing so much as to become ornaments to the profession they have chosen. They will cheerfully perform even the severest duties of fatigue, but they can not support the idea that they with their commands are looked upon as the pack horses of the public, upon whose backs every thing of an offensive carriage is to be piled. Even the miserable squatter, who has fled thither to avoid some justly merited punishment, hesitates not to complain of the partial manner in which the labour of the soldiers is bestowed. Why do not our representatives in Congress have them sent to do this or that—perhaps to causeway a swamp, lying between him and some neighbouring offender against the laws. The representatives of the people of the United States are not unfriendly to the army, and were they informed of the nature of the service which it is now called upon to perform and of its baneful effects, there would be an immediate repeal of all acts authorizing the employment of soldiers upon duties not properly appertaining to the military profession.

Fort Snelling, July 15, 1831

The roster to which reference has been made affords proof of the equal distribution of duty, and the morning reports exhibit continuous and severe fatigues in getting in wood, building an Indian agency house, and making hay for the

137

subsistence of the public oxen (quartermaster) and the beeves belonging to the subsistence department.

Fort Crawford, July 20, 1831

I have had no review and inspection of this command, nor have I required any, for I found it so circumstanced that to have done so would have been attended with considerable delay, as there were several distant working parties that must have been called in, besides the circumstance of its putting a complete stop for several days to the progress of the work going on here, and that too without affording to me any further information than is possessed by everyone else, viz., that these companies, which like all others of the 1st Infantry were perhaps better drilled than any other companies in service, have lost much ground since they commenced the service of fort and barrack building. I wish things could have been otherwise and that [the] 1st Infantry could have been permitted to confine itself to its more legitimate duties and thus have preserved the high stand which it once occupied and which it anxiously desires again to attain.

The paper marked B will prove to you that nothing or but little in the way of instruction could have been done or can now be done. It shows that since August 15th, 1830 (and to no more distant date did I require a report), there has been at times not a man for duty, and that even to include the winter months the general average of men *for duty* does not exceed one fourth the number of those on extra daily duty, and further that of those reported for duty a large proportion was during the working months detailed for the day on some extra service such as boating, etc., etc. Colonel [Willoughby] Morgan has assured me that the only drills which he has had in his power to give to his command were during the nights last winter between the hours of retreat and tattoo whenever the weather would permit.[9]

Fort Mackinac, September 19, 1833

Service. Exact and properly distributed, it would seem, but too severe, the getting in of the necessary supply of wood alone imposing more fatigue upon the men than consists with the proper and more legitimate duties of the soldier. Wood should most assuredly be furnished by contract at all posts where contracts can be made if it be desired to afford to the soldier every opportunity to perfect himself in his duties, and at no post sooner than this, where the labour of obtaining it is so great.

Fort Winnebago, October 10, 1833

Lieutenant Colonel [Enos] Cutler, not being able to hire a private waiter even at the extravagant rate of $30 per month or in truth for any price, has like Brevet Major [Matthew M.] Payne at Fort Gratiot been forced to take a soldier from the line. No blame can here attach, the necessities of the case are paramount both to the law and the regulations.

Fort Crawford, October 15, 1833

In 1831 I had to dispense with a review and inspection of the troops of this garrison because ⅘ of them were either absent upon various working parties, in preparing materials for the erection of the barracks, or actually engaged upon the buildings, and such being even now the state of things I am

---

[9] Retreat was to be sounded or beat at sunset. Tattoo was to be beat at a later hour, specified according to the circumstances of season and place, after which no soldier was to be out of his tent or quarters. See Article 18, *General Regulations of the Army,* 1835, for a description of the various calls of the day.

forced again to dispense with an inspection sooner than retard at this advanced season of the year the completion of certain buildings that are much wanted and that might besides be materially injured if left uncovered during the winter months. The barracks erected here are certainly the best in the country, but they have as certainly been built at the cost, I may say, of one of the best regiments that we have ever had. No officer attached to the regiment is at all chargeable with the loss it has sustained; all were absolved from responsibility so soon as their commands were required to perform other than legitimate service. The morning report of today gives but 49 non-commissioned officers and privates for duty out of the five companies and yet notes 84 on extra or daily duty or on detached service, and this may be received as about the average number reported during the last three years. I will make no comment upon this. I would but request that a reference may be had to my former reports, in all of which something may be found expressive of my most decided dislike to the system of citizen soldier making. The soldier, it is true, is no longer required to cultivate the soil, but instead thereof he is compelled to build barracks and to cut roads, a still more severe and continuous service of fatigue.

Fort Snelling, August 17, 1834

Service. The utmost that an officer in command of a frontier post like this can do is to render the service equal. He can not make it easy where 800 or 1,000 cords of wood and many tons of hay are to be cut and brought in from a distance perhaps of several miles.

Fort Leavenworth, August 26, 1836

Instruction. More advanced than I expected to find. The

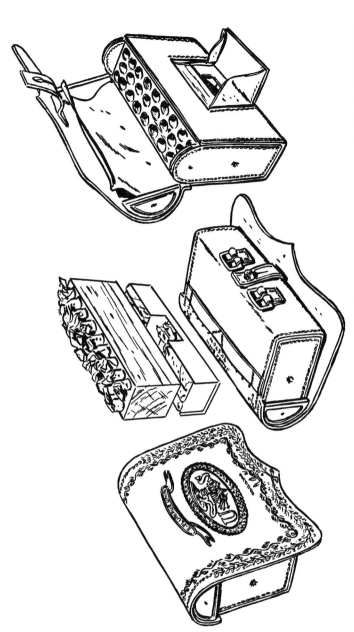

CARTRIDGE BOX, 1808–39

From a drawing by H. Charles McBarron, Jr.,
in *Small Arms and Ammunition in the United States Service*,
by Berkeley R. Lewis (Washington, 1956).

FORT BRADY
Both from *Vues et Souvenirs de l'Amérique du Nord,*
by Francis de Castelnau (Paris, 1842).

FORT MACKINAC

maneuvers which I required were executed in a very creditable manner. Colonel [Stephen W.] Kearny will, I am sure, leave no effort untried that can tend to the perfection of his regiment, and should any soldier who may have been under his immediate orders be discharged at the expiration of his term without having obtained a knowledge of the drill, it must be charged to the short period for which he was enlisted. The three years' enlistment is ruining the army.[10]

Fort Snelling, August 16, 1838

Service. Exact and regular and not more severe than has been at all times required at this post, where besides the ordinary fatigue duties the procurement of the necessary amount of hay, fire wood, etc., is devolved upon it. . . .

Instruction. Not much advanced. The old soldiers, it is true, are well practised in the drill and have the appearance and confident air of those satisfied with their proficiency in their particular arm, but they form so small a portion of the command that they can be noticed only as exceptions to the general charge of ignorance which I am bound to make.

Fort Winnebago, August 25, 1838

The company is pretty well drilled—much better than I had reason to expect, knowing that it was chiefly composed of recruits.

Fort Brady, September 12, 1838

Instruction. Not much advanced. Every effort is, however, now being made to instruct the soldier in the drill of the In-

[10] The reduction of the enlistment period from five to three years in 1833 was one part of an act "to improve the condition of the non-commissioned officers and privates of the army and marine corps of the United States and to prevent desertion." *United States Statutes at Large,* IV, 647.

fantry and Light Infantry. It might be well in this place to remark that not only are most of the men of the company recruits, but they are moreover not naturalized citizens of the United States—out of 52 composing the company, there are 32 foreigners, some of whom speak the English language so imperfectly as scarcely to be understood.[11]

Fort Leavenworth, July, 1840

This battalion is not so perfect in the drill as the five companies of the regiment were found to be on my inspection of them at this place in July, 1838. Colonel Kearny is fully sensible of this; in truth, he made known to me and accurately the state and condition of both men and horses before I saw them paraded for inspection. In a very short time a very great change must be wrought in the way of improvement, for Colonel Kearny is now as he has ever been, unwearied and active in his efforts to promote the efficiency of his command. It will be borne in mind that three of the companies present have but recently come from the Arkansas, where from the nature of their service but little time could be devoted to the drill, and further that out of more than one hundred recruits lately gained, fifty-five had received but little if any instruction. I speak of the battalion collectively—were I to pass upon that portion of it only which was inspected in 1838, it would doubtless be in praise.

[11] From 1820 to the Civil War a large proportion of the soldiers in the United States Army were of foreign birth, as a result of the difficulty in procuring suitable recruits from among the native born. In 1822 and 1823 roughly one-fourth of the men who enlisted were of foreign birth; in 1836 and 1837 the proportion was approximately 40 per cent. Of 5,000 recruits entering the service in 1850 and 1851, over 70 per cent were Europeans. Irish and Germans predominated among these foreign recruits. Registers of Enlistment, Adjutant General's Office, National Archives; Surgeon General's Office, *Statistical Report . . . from January, 1839, to January, 1855*, 626–28.

Jefferson Barracks, August, 1840

This regiment is better officered than any other in our service, and as it has never been called upon to perform any other than duties purely military since the first moment of its organization, I took it for granted that it had reaped the full benefit of those advantages, nor have I been disappointed. It is decidedly the best drilled corps that I have ever seen. The two battalions of the 1st Infantry, when under the command of Majors Twiggs and Kearny respectively, maneuvered as Infantry perhaps as well if not better, but as they were not well practiced in the exercise of Light Infantry, they can not be said to have been so well instructed as this regiment is at this time, for it is equally well skilled in either the Infantry or Light Infantry tactics.

Fort Snelling, September, 1840

Service. I can not doubt of its correctness nor hesitate to admit that it has been and is occasionally a little severe. The getting in of 12 or 1,400 cords of wood from a distance of five or six miles is of itself quite a task for two companies, but independently of this, much labour has been bestowed by the command upon the walls of the fort and upon the quarters of both officers and men.

Fort Winnebago, July 5, 1842

In Infantry drill there is much room for improvement before it can reach the point to which it once attained, but I hope and expect much from the apparent desire of the officers to recover as soon as possible all that has been lost. Many uninstructed recruits have joined since April last, and it is but justice to state that the company has all along been upon fatigue duties in the winter getting in fire wood, and since the opening of the spring in various necessary labours about the fort. The renewal of the fences around the public grounds (parade, gardens, stable yards, etc.) required 9,000 posts and rails, and to get them alone cost both time and labour.

Fort Snelling, July 16, 1842

The getting of wood, at all times a serious matter, will become every year more tedious and difficult of accomplishment. At this moment no good wood can be obtained short of 8 or 10 miles from the fort. But I know not that a change for the better in the mode of getting wood can be expected; hard as the duty is upon the soldier, ever anxious as we all are to relieve him from it, I question whether he would choose to effect it at the cost which would be brought about were the supply furnished by contract.

Fort Snelling, September 3, 1843

There is a very decided improvement in the drill since my last inspection; still it falls short of that exactness which was witnessed at Jefferson Barracks. If it be asked, why is this, it may be answered that the long winters and necessary fatigue consume so much of the year as to leave scarcely three months to be devoted to military exercises. 45 days have just been consumed in procuring 500 tons of hay and perhaps 90 more are now to be given towards the getting in of 1,200 cords of fire wood. Captain [Electus] Backus assures me that when his command was drilled every day (as it was prior to the commencement of hay making), it was more perfect than it is at present, and this we must believe and the rather, as during the interruption of the drill the men were engaged in occupations directly at variance with the proper duties of the soldier.

144

Fort Atkinson, September 7, 1843

Service. Regular and at this moment by no means severe, for the work being completed, fatigue duties will not become heavy until the winter, when the procurement of wood will prove a serious task.

Fort Towson, June 4, 1844

For the last 18 months the average number of men on extra and daily duty has not fallen short of 120, so that unless on Sunday no battalion drills could be had. The men therefore are better practised in the company than the battalion drill. They, however, march correctly and in time, much more so than I had a right to expect when informed of the character of their fatigue duties.

Fort Des Moines, July 25, 1845

The step and movements generally of the company are not so precise and exact as I could wish, showing evidently that a further schooling is necessary to better instruction in the drill. The men perfectly understand how every movement should be made, but from want of practise perhaps have either lost or never acquired the proper time and precision of step necessary to their exact performance. The company is somewhat practised in the Light Infantry drill, and some members of it are tolerably well instructed in the school of the field piece, as fully perhaps as may be necessary to meet any calls that may be made upon them, at least in the Indian country.

About two months since, Lieutenant [Robert S.] Granger arrived to take charge of the company, and immediately on assuming the command of it, he recommenced the drills, which had been for some time virtually suspended owing to

145

the ill health of the subaltern whom he succeeded, and continued them daily until the dews became so heavy and the weather so hot as to render it unsafe to expose his command to their influence. I mention this circumstance in justice to the men, who, I am sure, with equal opportunities would soon become as well instructed as any other members of the 1st Infantry. I would have it borne in mind, too, that 19 men of the company were enlisted during the last year and did not join until November.

Fort Crawford, August 12, 1845

The manual of the field piece is sufficiently understood and practised to enable the commanding officer to have salutes fired when necessary in proper time and without fear of accident.

Fort Mackinac, August 23, 1845

The command is pretty well instructed, but it is apparent that Company C has been more frequently exercised in battalion than the company of the 5th, and yet its step is not more precise or exact than theirs. Even the best drilled companies, if unaccustomed to battalion evolutions, are apt to commit faults if not mistakes, and they are first detected when the march is in column in the failure to preserve distances and the direction and to have the front of subdivisions square with the line of direction. None of the companies have of late been much practised as skirmishers, although they are by no means ignorant of the drill, and I may say here and with regret that few of the regiments have, since the introduction of the present system, shown that fondness for Light Infantry exercise which was once so prevalent.

APPEARANCE UNDER ARMS

Nothing pleased the old soldier Croghan more than a fine appearance of the soldiers on parade, and a special section of each report was reserved for his comments on "Appearance under Arms." He found a great variety. Some commands had the sharp appearance he delighted to see. The men were good-looking specimens, uniform in size, and quick and graceful in their movements. But others were awkward and unmilitary, their appearance to be explained by a number of factors—the large proportion of recent recruits, for example, or of immigrants who could understand little English. Croghan's tone was not so much one of censure as of disappointment that the army had to rely on such poor stock to man its regiments.

Fort Gibson, August, 1827

Appearance of the men under arms—soldier-like with the exception of Captain [Nathaniel G.] Wilkinson's company, in which there are a few men who will never perhaps acquire either the feelings or the proper deportment of the true soldier; and it is not often otherwise. Men educated for one of the learned professions never enlist until they become un-fitted for any useful life, particularly for that of the soldier.

Fort Crawford, August 20, 1838

The men of the command are of ordinary stature and personally as good looking as we had reason to expect from the almost unlimited authority which has been recently given with regard to enlistments.

Fort Leavenworth, July, 1840

When mounted and fully caparisoned, the appearance is by no means so fine as I have been accustomed to see in the companies of this regiment, many of the horses being in miserable plight, the arms and equipments of different patterns and in too many instances much defaced and worn. Colonel Kearny is by no means answerable for this condition of things. That the horses of E, G, and K companies are in such bad order must be ascribed to the fact of their having been badly fed and entirely exposed to the inclemencies of the weather during several months on the Arkansas, from whence they have been recently brought. As to the arms and equipments, let the proper department bear the blame (if blame there be) of having furnished them of different patterns. The Colonel can very easily prove that they are not more worn or defaced than might be expected from the nature of the service to which he has necessarily exposed them. The men themselves are pretty good looking, though some six or eight are not well suited to Dragoon service, instance one man of six feet four and weighing 250 pounds; what horse could carry such a monster?

But even were there the greatest lack of soldierly appearance I would not rest thereon my chief objection to a portion of this command. Personal appearance it is true is something, but it is much more to have men who can understand you and whom you can understand. Out of a detachment of recruits consisting of one hundred and ten received a few weeks ago, there are perhaps twenty who neither understand nor speak a word of English. They are either Dutch or Germans. It is no pleasant task to instruct raw recruits, but when those recruits are ignorant of your language, the task becomes ten times more tedious and disagreeable. I would suggest the propriety of forbidding the enlistment of all such persons for the future, taking care at the same time to issue a like interdict against the Irish, who (a few honourable exceptions to the contrary) are the very bane of our garrisons.[12]

Jefferson Barracks, August, 1840

The men generally, having been compelled to leave behind at Green Bay their dress uniforms in the hurry of their march to the Winnebago country, do not in consequence appear to the best advantage. They are, however, good looking and of proper size and have too that stern and soldier-like aspect which is almost invariably noticed in those who, having confidence in their officers, are at the same time not without a self-assurance in their own ability to play well the parts that may be allotted to them.

Fort Crawford, September, 1840

The men of this command have been almost entirely corrected of that sluggish, clownish gait and figure which invariably mark the recruit and now present a fine soldier-like appearance.

Fort Winnebago, July 5, 1842

There are many foreigners in this company, Germans principally, men of homely, stolid-looking visages but of stout frame well becoming the dress and equipments of the soldier, and the whole as a body, being very nearly of the same height, makes a very fine appearance.

Jefferson Barracks, August, 1843

I know not that any single company separately considered is better looking than that of the 1st at Fort Leavenworth, but certainly the brigade when formed in line exhibited a very imposing appearance in which the eye was unable to detect those defects which more immediately discover themselves in smaller bodies of men. I think, however, that both

12 See footnote 11 above.

efficiency and appearance would be materially promoted were pains taken to secure to each company men of uniform height and not have assignment made as hitherto without regard to size, thus attaching not unfrequently to the same squad men of 6 feet 2 or more inches with some of 5 feet 4 or less.

Fort Atkinson, September 7, 1843

The company of Dragoons is among the finest looking that I have seen, being composed of men above the ordinary height and of very soldier-like appearance whether mounted or on foot. The Infantry company has much improved in appearance since I last remarked upon it, but its strength is so reduced, being 19 only for duty, that although well dressed and equipped in the neatest possible manner and consisting in truth of good looking men, it suffers in comparison with the Dragoon company from the very smallness of its numbers.

RECRUITING

The supply of soldiers for the army came largely from the eastern centers of population, and Croghan did not frequently come in contact with the serious problem of recruiting men who were suitable in quality and adequate in number. When his inspection tour carried him to a recruiting rendezvous, however, he was able to set down on paper his observations and suggestions. They exhibit his usual practical wisdom.

Recruiting Rendezvous, Louisville, April 27, 1827

This officer has succeeded very well; he has within the last ten days sent off a detachment of recruits to the general depot at Jefferson Barracks, and it has since then enlisted 15 men, young and sturdy looking fellows. The house which he occupies as a barracks is a comfortable one, sufficiently roomy and located in the suburb of the town, a fortunate circumstance alike for the recruit and citizens of the place. The recruits have learned but little or nothing, as might be expected, and even yet retain a spatter of the canal mud out of which they were taken. The regulations expect much from a recruit, greatly more than can be obtained or ought to be aimed at where success in enlisting is the main object of desire.

At a recruiting rendezvous nothing should be attempted that might, even by a possibility, dissatisfy the recruit or deter those around from enlisting. Pay strict attention to messing, cleanliness of person and of quarters, and nothing more; as for the schools of the soldier and company, leave them to be practised at the general depot, to which place the recruit ought to be sent as soon as possible. I am convinced that the recruiting service must continue to suffer so long as a strict observance of the 1293rd paragraph of General Regulations is exacted of the recruiting officers.[13] The first lessons of the soldier are disgusting to the recruit; a call to them is like a summons to the stocks, and that looker-on who should afterwards listen to this report of his annoyance and suffering and then enlist must have more than ordinary hardihood. So much depends upon the recruiting sergeant at every rendezvous that to ensure those of intelligence and worthy of trust, I would recommend that an order be issued directing that whenever a detail for the recruiting service is made, every officer designated shall be attended to the post ap-

[13] The paragraph read in part: "The instruction of recruits will commence from the moment of enlistment, as well to provide against the vices of idleness, as to qualify them to join some regiment. In general, and under favourable circumstances, two months ought to suffice to make them acquainted with the first duties of police, and the schools of the soldier and company, in infantry tactics." Paragraph 1293, Article 74, *General Regulations for the Army,* 1825.

pointed to him by a non-commissioned officer of his own selection out of the company in which he himself has been serving. Emulation among the non-commissioned officers at all the military posts would be thus created, and as a consequence those of good character only would in a little time be found at the several recruiting rendezvous; and at an additional stimulus to exertion, let one or two dollars be paid to them for each recruit sent to the general depot.

Depot orders directing the discharge of non-commissioned officers and soldiers on certificates of disability for service are not so particular as to be of the least service to the recruiting officer. . . . To guard against the impositions which are frequently practised upon the recruiting officer by those who have been previously discharged on certificates of disability, all orders for discharge should not only give a precise personal description of those discharged, but also an accurate delineation of the injuries or diseases under which they were severally discharged. Among the number of disabilities habitual drunkenness is received, and upon the surgeon's certificate to this effect discharges have in consequence been granted. This is wrong, if for this reason alone, that he who may be discontented with the service has but to choose between a continuance in it and an envolvement among the number of habitual drunkards, either in fact or under pretence. In 1825 (the anecdote has been related to me by an officer of the 3rd Infantry) a man belonging to the company of Brevet Major [John] Bliss was discharged at Fort Howard as an habitual drunkard; the discharge once obtained, the man drank no more and very soon after hired himself to the sutler of the post and began to work at his former trade of tailor.

Fort Armstrong, July 1, 1827

Before leaving this part of the Mississippi, I would suggest the propriety of establishing a recruiting rendezvous for the 5th Regiment at Galena (Fever River); there are many stout looking fellows about there who, disappointed in the expectation of rapid gain in working of the mines, would be glad to enlist as soldiers sooner than return empty handed to their former homes. Such at all events is the opinion of those of the village with whom I have conversed on the subject.

THE OFFICERS

The routine reports of Croghan do not devote much attention to the officers as a group. Words of praise or criticism appear usually in connection with the duties for which they were responsible, but once in a while Croghan devotes some special remarks to relations between the officers. He gives us a glimpse into the stresses and strains that accompanied life at a wilderness outpost.

Fort Snelling, August, 1826

That harmony so desirable at every post and especially so at a frontier one seems not to prevail here. The officer in command and some of his junior officers are at variance. He gives his orders; they obey them, though not without some grumbling and questioning of their correctness. There is an enforcement of subordination and thus far there is discipline agreeably to the construction of the term as given in the book of regulations. Reports made to me with respect to the habits of Brevet Major [Thomas] Hamilton of this regiment and post fix upon him the character of a confirmed sot, and my own personal observations since my recent introduction to him serve not to convince me of their incorrectness. Consider what I now say, however, only as corroborative of what you may have previously heard in relation to the Major. I hope that I may be mistaken in the impressions which I have received, at all events that the case may be viewed leniently. He has a large and interesting family; he is poor; he is old and has seen long service.

Fort Snelling, May, 1827

I regret to state that dissensions still prevail between Colonel [Josiah] Snelling and some of his junior officers, even to a greater extent than was remarked upon in my last report. Lieutenant [David] Hunter, who has been under arrest for some months, is now confined to his quarters for reasons best known to Colonel Snelling, of the propriety of which I will not venture a remark as it will doubtless shortly be passed upon by a court martial. I do not, however, commit myself in saying that each of the parties (Colonel Snelling and Lieutenant Hunter) believes himself to be correct. May it not, therefore, be that neither is morally wrong. Lieutenant Hunter is young and perhaps of a temper too warm and unyielding, and Colonel Snelling, sometimes irascible, may have in the moment of excitement, produced by some official anxiety, unguardedly expressed himself in language calculated to wound his feelings. Sympathy is expressed by most of the officers of the garrison, not, it may be, that he is believed to be unjustly arrested and confined, but because his confinement has been long and may prove injurious to his health. It is to be regretted that Mr. Hunter has not ere this been brought before a court martial. Odium will most generally attach to the person ordering an arrest when the party arrested is for a long time and to all appearance unnecessarily deprived of the benefit of a trial, be the criminality of the party arrested as positive as it may and the efforts of the arresting officer to obtain a court as persevering and urgent as the utmost latitude of proper subordination can warrant.

Baton Rouge Arsenal, May, 1829

Lieutenant Adams, who certainly has taste and a great deal of industry, has made for himself a fine garden beautifully set off with a handsome fish pond, with a bathing house, bridge, etc., altogether so far exceeding anything about Baton Rouge that they have become perhaps too frequently the subjects of remark. That all this has been done at the Lieutenant's own expence does not alter his case; the censorious will talk. It will be said he spends too much money, his allowances from the government are too great and should be reduced, etc. An officer can not truly call his *own money his own*, for should he choose to purchase a costly article of uniform even, the fault finders would be upon him forthwith, and the consequence might be a reduction of the pay of the whole army. As to the fish pond, I would have it remain by all means because it would be valuable in case of a fire, and it is besides ornamental and not endangering to the health of the place. I mention this because there is talk about draining it.

Fort Des Moines, October 26, 1836

The company which, as I before observed, is under orders to proceed to Fort Leavenworth is filled exclusively by selection from the entire command of such soldiers as have not less than twelve months to serve. It having departed, the garrison will then consist of the lieutenant colonel commanding, a captain, and a subaltern, with scarcely men enough to attend to the stable duties, as there will be many surplus horses requiring their care. And what will be the strength of this command by or before the close of next April? 18 rank and file. Every other enlistment will by that time have terminated, and of the officers it is believed that the lieutenant colonel alone will be willing to remain in service after the commencement of the spring. I have been often asked why so many resignations, and my reply has invariably been, I know not.[14] I am fully aware that there is much dissatisfaction and that hence so many resignations, but whence such dissatisfaction is only to be conjectured by me, for I have made no inquiries into the matter. One thing is certain, however; where there is discontent among the officers, it will extend itself to the men, and that so long as it does prevail, so long will the ranks of our regiments be kept thin.

Fort Winnebago, August 25, 1838

Lieutenant [Isaac] Lynde is the only company officer at the post—and upon him is devolved the duties of commandant of a company, acting quartermaster, commissary of subsistence, standing officer of the day, adjutant of the post, keeper of the post fund, and director of the bake house.

Fort Snelling, July 16, 1842

I cannot perceive any want of proper discipline; order and content seem to prevail throughout, and it is pleasing to witness the harmony which extends among the several families of the post, the members of which seem to vie with each other in efforts to promote the comfort and enjoyment of the whole.

---

[14] The number of resignations struck the editor of the *Army and Navy Chronicle* as an "appalling sight to look upon." He attributed the resignations largely to the insufficient pay. *Army and Navy Chronicle*, Vol. II (1836), 313; Vol. III (1836), 313; Vol. VI (1838), 8.

SOLDIERS IN UNIFORM
From Plate XVII, "Artillery, Infantry, Dragoon (Full Dress),
1835–1850," a lithograph by H. A. Ogden, in *The Army
of the United States* (Washington, 1888).

FORT LEAVENWORTH IN 1849

JEFFERSON BARRACKS
From *The Valley of the Mississippi,*
by J. C. Wild (St. Louis, 1841).

6: INDIAN AFFAIRS

INTIMATELY connected with the military posts of the West was the question of Indian policy and Indian relations. It was only natural, then, that the Indians should come within the scope of the Inspector General's observations. While not officially responsible for the state of Indian relations, Croghan could not pass over entirely the chance to voice his opinions about the system of Indian traders, the Indian agents, and the treaties made with the red men. The best statement of his views came at the end of his inspection career, when he appended to his report of 1845 some detailed remarks on Indian questions.

Fort Brady, July 9, 1826
Lieutenant Colonel [William] Lawrence is at variance with the Indian agent, Mr. [Henry R.] Schoolcraft, growing out of the operation of the 1146th Number, 72d Article of the Rules and Regulations of the Army, as was the officer whom he relieved in the command of the post from the same cause.[1] I do sincerely hope that there will either be an entire recision of this 1146 or such alterations made in it as to allow officers in command of posts some discretionary power in relation to

[1] *"Issues to Indians.*—Issues to Indians will be made on returns signed by the commanding officer or Indian agent—a separate abstract will be made by the assistant-commissary, signed by the commanding officer, which will be entered in the monthly return of provisions received and issued." Paragraph 1146, Article 72, *General Regulations for the Army,* 1825.

157

issues of subsistence. I fear that the best feelings do not generally prevail, nor will they under existing circumstances, when Indian agents have the same control over certain stores at posts as the military officers in command themselves have, and can at will obtain orders directing those commanding officers to erect for them with the soldiers under their command quarters, etc., etc., with soldiers perhaps already worn down by long continued fatigue in the preparation of their own. Among the last military orders which I received at New Orleans previous to my resignation in 1817 was one directing me to send a detachment from my command to some place in the Creek country to report to an Indian agent for whom it was to build houses; and forsooth, I received a severe written reprimand for not having sent him better men. In stating to you as in duty bound the feelings of the officers here in relation to the subject, I may be indulging my own personal ones too far. I will therefore conclude by expressing a hope that ere long military and Indian affairs may be kept as distinct as it is to be wished the military and civil ever may be.

Jefferson Barracks, September, 1827

Before proceeding further, I would return upon a portion of the route which I have travelled over. A post of one company to be drawn from Cantonment Jesup might be properly placed about midway between that place and Cantonment Towson, say near the Caddo agency or at the post recently vacated, about 25 miles above—(its name not remembered).[2] This position is not taken up with exclusive relation to the proper line of defence of the Red River but with equal reference to the agency, which like all others can not exist among

[2] Possibly the post at Sulphur Fork, established in 1817 and evacuated in 1824.

the frontier Indians in proper consideration without the immediate countenance and support of a military force. The Caddos and other Indians of that agency are in the strictest terms of commercial intercourse with the Comanches and other tribes of Texas. How soon this friendly intercourse may be interrupted can not be determined, unless by the application of the rule "that Indian treaties seldom last long"—and what might be the effect of open rupture I am not prepared to determine. It can not, however, be fraught with less than great distress to the settlements.

On the upper Red River, that is to say, about and above the Spanish Bluffs on the west side, are found the Choctaws, Pottawatamies, Wecas, Kickapoos, a few of the Lower Creeks, and remains of other tribes not recollected, invited thither by the hope of good hunting, in which I fear they have been disappointed, for their extreme distress for food and the scarcity of game was the common talk among the whites with whom I stopped. Want will very soon dispose them to join in any enterprise, however daring and desperate, that may hold out even in remote view a prospect of altering their present condition. At this moment there is quiet even among themselves because the extremity is not yet arrived, but when arrived—and arrive it must, the cattle of the frontier settlements must stand in place of the buffalo, elk, and deer, of which they have been deprived. I would earnestly recommend the establishment of a military post between Cantonments Gibson and Leavenworth, and the point that I would fix upon is on the Niosho River in the immediate neighbourhood of the village of the Osage chief, White Hair, and about midway between the Missouri and Arkansas Rivers. . . .

The immediate object that I have in view in the erection of this post is the preservation of the Osages—for without it they are doubly at the mercy of the Pawnees, their deadly enemies, who, being much stronger, can not only strike them when they please, but cut them off from the buffalo hunt— almost their exclusive means of support. The Osages possess a country as may be seen by the map of but 50 miles base running back to the Rocky Mountains, but of what value to them is the claim which they set up to a greater portion of this surface, for if they advance even within a day's ride of good hunting ground, they risk an encounter with the present occupants—the Pawnees.

The abandonment of Council Bluffs will prove the destruction of the whole Osage tribe, unless some military position be taken in their country by our troops to prevent the incursions of the Pawnees. Some of the Pawnee villages are within a short ride of Council Bluffs, and during the occupancy of that place we said, "Strike the Osages, and we strike you," and they were afraid; but they fear no longer; they believe that, convinced of our weakness, we have shrunk back from the imposing strength of the Pawnees, and they will not act without dread of consequences.

Should two companies be stationed on the Niosho, let one be mounted and armed as heavy cavalry; no other description of force is in that country fitted for more than the mere routine of garrison service. An infantry man might as well be sent to chase the elk or deer as to pursue the Osage or Pawnee of the Plains—as was exemplified in August last at Cantonment Gibson. One white man was killed and another wounded within three miles of the post. The wounded man escaped but was chased to the river and within gun shot of the fort. Immediate pursuit was given by an entire company, but as a matter of course without effect. Give also one if not two companies of cavalry to both Cantonment Gibson and

Leavenworth; then, if the officers at those posts be at all vigilant, the peace of the whole frontier from Prairie du Chien to Cantonment Jesup will be secured, or I am much mistaken in the character of the Indians.

The Indian agents have much in their power from the influence which they can command over the Indians, but they do not act in such concert as to be of much use unless as to mere distribution of presents and annuities, and even this service they sometimes perform without due regard to the wishes of the government, which are in favor of an *equal* distribution without any reference to the rank or influence of particular Indians. Their very appointments are in themselves improperly worded; instead of being commissioned "of the Indian Department" without reference to a particular tribe, each is appointed to an individual agency. The consequence is that interested feelings too frequently govern; the man becomes identified with the tribe, and the jealousies of the tribe become his. I have observed this, and it has been observed by more than me.

There are between Cantonment Jesup and the Missouri five Indian agents . . . and what do they know of the acts of each other? Nothing—they are as if they were the jealous chiefs of the tribes over which they exercise guardianship and, because they enquire not, view every act of their neighbours through a false and prejudged medium. But what would I have them do? Let a constant correspondence in relation to the several tribes be kept up, and, that it might be made appear to the Indians that an interest in their welfare was really felt by those who stand in the light of their guardians, let a grand camp fire or congress be held once a year or oftener at one of those agencies. The congress to consist of the several agents themselves, the nearest military commandants,

161

the three principal chiefs and three delegates from each tribe, for the adjustment of differences and to deliberate upon the state of affairs of each tribe, with the means of bettering them. Let the proceedings of the council at each meeting be reduced to writing by an official secretary and signed by each one present, that they may be read at the next stated meeting. But will the wisest deliberations at these councils relieve present distress? No. They will serve, however, to ensure peace among themselves and secure the repose of the frontiers, great points gained; and may in the end instruct the government as to the best means to be pursued for the permanent relief and establishment of these unfortunate people.

There are two missionary establishments among the Osages, at one of which, the Harmony mission on the Osage River, I remained during two days and was much pleased at the zeal in behalf of the Indians that was manifested by the Elder— the Reverend Mr. Dodge and his assistants, but I much fear that in spite of their efforts to evangelize, but little progress has been made. Their school consists of 40 or 45 scholars of both sexes and between the ages of eight and thirteen; most of them can spell, read, and write quite well and have some idea of geography. Of the half breeds, whose white parents take interest in their well doing, something may be expected, but the case is widely different with those of Indian parents, who can never be weaned from their wild life so long as they are in daily habit of free communion with those of their tribe. The Osage sends his child to school because the game is scarce and he has but little meat to give him, but if the next hunt be a good one, he is taken home again, where his advancement in book learning is not only not estimated, but the very scholar himself is ridiculed for his awkwardness, and he indeed feels that he has been degraded.

162

The policy pursued of late years by the government in relation to the Indians is at war with the very idea of civilizing them. It is literally turning out the tame fawn to the wild herd. Something might have been done with those broken bands on the Red River had they been left at their native homes, but what can now be expected of them?—nothing— the less civilized and more savage they become, the greater will be their chance of obtaining the means of support.

Fort Atkinson, September 7, 1843

Governor [John] Chambers of this Territory, being duly empowered by the Secretary of War, has directed Captain [Edwin V.] Sumner to remove the Winnebagoes that may be on the Mississippi River or in its vicinity to the neutral ground, and he will proceed to act in obedience to his instructions on the 15th instant should they refuse to obey their agent, Mr. [David] Lowry, who has called upon them to leave the Mississippi, as not until they do will he pay them a cent of their present annuity. Should they prove obstinate, the Captain will have a delicate and responsible duty to perform, for remove them he must, such are his instructions, even though he have to resort to force, and when removed some will return to their old haunts and thus render it necessary to keep up a constant patrol, to the great annoyance of the Dragoons and certainly not to their benefit.

These Indians are in no amiable mood just now; still I can not think that they will remain where they are beyond the stipulated time. None of them will, I am sure, unless designing men introduce whiskey among them and thus lead them openly to defy their agent and perhaps to commit outrages that might end in blood.

The present discontent among them has grown out of several causes, the most prominent of which are the determination of the government to confine them to the neutral ground, which does not furnish game enough for their subsistence, a cruel and unnecessary measure as they conceive, for in fishing and hunting about the Mississippi they can not trespass upon anyone's rights; the violation of treaty stipulations in withholding $1,200 of this year's annuity and applying it to the payment of an unjust claim; and the instructions of the Indian Department at Washington to the traders to grant no more credits, a complete bar (if the traders obey) to their fall and winter hunts, their only sources of profit. On the credits given they obtain traps, powder, lead, blankets, and other articles of clothing and out of the proceeds of the hunt they pay off their credits, in whole or part depending upon the goodness of the hunt. I am not objecting to this order of the Indian Department, for I think it a good one. I only speak of it because it is viewed by the Indians as a further evidence of the desire of the whites to drive them to the wall. The Winnebagoes are bad in all conscience, but they have certainly been badly used in the course of the last fifteen years.

Any further remarks of mine on the subject of these Indians would be needless if not out of place, as you are already without doubt well informed of the true state of the case between us and them.

Fort Atkinson, August 9, 1845

That proper discipline prevails must be inferred from the promptness and apparent cheerfulness with which orders are obeyed, and from the fact that the morning report book shows so few marks in the column headed "in confinement." In the guard house there is not a soldier, but unfortunately there are five Winnebago Indians, confined for killing the cattle of some citizen of the Territory. Major [Greenleaf] Dearborn is aware that in thus confining them he acts with the strong hand and illegally, but how can he act otherwise? Should he refuse to punish those who commit such outrages by confining them on bread and water for a time, they would escape punishment altogether, for the citizen upon whom the outrage was committed would sooner bear the loss than go to the expence of taking the matter before the courts, which may possibly be 100 miles distant from his place of residence.

Milwaukee, August 20, 1845

I did intend at one time to address a special communication to you on the subject of our Indian relations, but having become doubtful of my ability to give it value, I have changed my purpose and instead thereof will append to this inspection report now completed a few notes and observations made with reference to my original intention, which will be taken by you at what they may be worth.

Licensed Indian traders. Indian traders have great control over the tribes among which or with which they conduct their trade, far exceeding that possessed by even the most popular of the government agents, who in fact are not heeded by the Indians when they would urge anything in opposition to the wishes of the traders. The sooner this fact is known in Washington and acted upon the better, that we may enlist in behalf of the government the most active aid in all our dealings with the Indians instead of having it operate in opposition to our wishes and with effect. Confound not together the licensed trader and the whiskey dealer of the frontier. The latter is but the unprincipled scoundrel who makes the Indian drunk that he may rob him of his blanket, rifle, traps, and whatever else he can lay his hands on. The former, on the contrary, refuses the Indian whiskey, urges him to leave the settlement of the whites, at the same time providing him with needful articles and in every way encouraging him to exert himself in the hunt, well knowing that they are mutually and gainfully interested in its result. The trader (the intelligent and well informed of course I mean) should in every case be consulted whenever a treaty is to be made, first because without his aid we can not deal with the Indians, and again because his true interests instead of warring with those of the Indians are in fact alike and unopposed.

A recent act of Congress declares in effect that no treaty made for the future with the Indians shall provide for the payment of debts due by them to traders, but that the Indians shall be themselves the recipients of whatever sum or sums of money or goods may be secured to them by treaty. Mark the operation of this law. The Indian, being the immediate recipient of whatever may properly fall to his share and which may far exceed his present wants, forthwith disposes of the excess to the whiskey dealer for whiskey, and in a little while after, everything that he has received, money, blankets, and all being wasted in riot and drunkenness, and he poor devil, driven out and denied even the least assistance by the wretch who has robbed him, returns at last to the trader by whom he has been so often relieved but who has been virtually told not to supply his wants, press as they may. I will present two instances strongly contrasting with each other, among the many that might be brought forward, in proof of what I assert and in favor of a different system of payment from the one usually adopted.

The first—[Jean Baptiste] Faribault of St. Peters, a regular and licensed trader, has been for years in the habit of crediting Little Six's band of the Sioux to the full amount of their annuity, some 17 or $1,800, and at the pay table the whole amount is turned over to him by the agent (in the presence and by consent of the Indians); thus not even a cent passes into the hands of the Indians, in other words into the clutches of the whiskey dealer. Faribault, knowing their proper wants, provides for those only, and thus a trade is carried on alike profitable to both parties; he makes a handsome profit on the sale of the goods, and they by having their purchases confined to actual necessaries are now doing comparatively well in every respect.

The second—Little Crow's band, occupying a village on the Mississippi 6 or 8 miles below Fort Snelling, but a few years ago ranked among the foremost in point of respectability of all the Sioux tribes; now it is reduced to the lowest depth of degradation, disunity, debauched, and poverty stricken, and all through the agency of the whiskey dealers. It is the recipient of its own annuity and most frequently receiving it when it least needs it (for what cares an Indian for extra blankets in August), every individual member, as might be expected, very soon passes the river to barter all away for whiskey and gewgaws.

Mr. [T. Hartley] Crawford of the Indian bureau at Washington is of opinion that it would be better were the Indian annuities paid in more goods and less money—in this I differ from him. Take the case of Faribault just stated; he gives a credit to the full amount of the annuity to the band for which he is a licensed trader, not at once, but only at such times as the necessary wants of the different families may demand it, thus supplying everyone with articles of use and at the same time depriving all of the means of traffic for whiskey—at least of those to be derived from the annuity. And such would be the case with other bands and other traders were all annuities paid in money, a proper system of credits established, and the present restrictions with respect to debts to traders in some degree removed. But what takes place under existing circumstances, where large amounts of goods are paid over as part of an annuity. The Indian receiving in the month of August most probably a store of blankets, woolen cloth, etc., for his family or for himself, careless of tomorrow and thinking not about the winter, sells them to the whiskey dealer, often times a blanket for a quart of whiskey, and lies about in drunken broils and riot until he has nothing left to barter, and when at last forced by sheer want to go upon his hunt, it must prove a very good one indeed if it furnish him subsistence and at the same time supply him with skins enough from the sale of which to purchase back at five dollars the very blanket which he before bartered for a quart of *Indian whiskey,* a poison made by compounding together bad whiskey, water, tobacco juice, and red pepper.

The whiskey dealers, getting their supplies as we have seen at prices nominal merely, are thus enabled so far to undersell the regular traders as to compel some of them to leave the Indian country to seek elsewhere a livelihood and in some instances to take upon themselves the more profitable calling of whiskey dealers. My remarks are here made with exclusive reference to the traders, Indians, and whiskey dealers of the Missouri and Mississippi rivers and their tributaries, but they may possibly apply with equal truth and propriety to many of those on the lakes and southern rivers.

Indian agents. Indian agents should not be appointed to any particular agency or tribe of Indians, but commissioned of the Indian department and liable for duty in whatever place it might be thought best to station them. In this way the Secretary of War could at any time command the best talents of

168

the whole number to carry into effect any particular measure. In few cases is it safe to appoint as agent a person resident of the vicinity in which a vacancy may happen or be created, as sectional feelings and prejudices as well as personal interests are almost sure to govern and not unfrequently to the injury of both whites and Indians. He who is fit for the place of Indian agent at all is equally well qualified for an agency whether at the north or the south, the Indian character being the same throughout.

The pay of agents ought to be increased 50 per cent at least, and vacant agencies should be filled by promoting the most deserving sub agents.

The old factory system[3] is a favorite one with some persons, but not with me, and instead of recommending a return to it, I would suggest a change in the present course of the trade (at least with a certain portion of the Indian tribes) that I have within the last few years more than once pointed out to intelligent traders and others well versed in Indian matters, and in every instance to the confirmation of my opinion in its entire fitness. The plan I propose is this—

Appoint a trader to every tribe of Indians receiving annuities from our government, excepting only the more educated and civilized southern tribes. The appointment to be made by the Secretary of War, but in every case of the person

[3] The factory system was an attempt of the federal government to regulate the Indian trade with justice to both Indians and whites. Beginning in 1796, government factories or trading posts were set up throughout the South and West, but opposition of independent traders and financial difficulties forced the liquidation of the program in 1822. Royal B. Way, "The United States Factory System for Trading with the Indians, 1796–1822," *Mississippi Valley Historical Review,* Vol. VI (1919), 220–35; Katherine Coman, "Government Factories; An Attempt to Control Competition in the Fur Trade," in *Papers and Discussions of the Twenty-third Annual Meeting of the American Economic Association,* 1910; Ora Brooks Peake, *A History of the United States Indian Factory System, 1795–1822* (Denver, 1954).

169

selected or chosen by the Indians themselves and approved by the agent of the tribe. The trader thus appointed shall be required by the agent to keep always on hand at some central or convenient place a complete stock of goods of the best quality and laid in at the lowest wholesale prices at the principal sea port cities, which he shall vend to the Indians agreeably to the tariff of prices fixed by the board—the board to consist of the agent, an army officer, and a citizen selected by the two. Once in every year the agent shall furnish the trader a roll of his tribe, particularly noting upon it the amount of annuity to be paid or due to each person or head of a family; from this the trader shall open an account with cash, taking care that every article sold be duly charged to the person who made the purchase. The books or accounts are once in every year to be submitted in the presence of a delegation of the tribe to the board above stated, and if they be found to be correct, a warrant or draft approved by the officer and citizen as members of the board may be drawn upon the Treasury by the agent in favor of the trader for the full amount of the credits, provided they exceed not the annuity.

Should the trader be appointed to an entire tribe, he shall be required to have ample stores of goods among all the principal bands of the tribes at such points as the agent may designate and at no other, and will be held strictly accountable that the persons appointed by him to vend them conform to the tariff and regulations established by the board. The advantage to accrue to the Indian from such a system would at once manifest itself to one at all conversant with their habits and informed as to the mode in which the annuities are sometimes paid.

No time for payment being specifically fixed, it not unfrequently happens that an entire band of distant Indians, acting under incorrect reports, assembles at the accustomed place of payment and after waiting there for weeks in a starving condition at last departs, to return again only to be again disappointed, and if perchance not disappointed, to barter away to miserable harpies perhaps there met together to fleece them their entire receipts, possibly not for whiskey but for something else of no real value to them.

Few of the Indians derive advantage from their annuities; many suffer from them, for the payment of them being made as just stated at no fixed time, they fritter away the most valuable season of the year either at their villages or the pay ground, afraid to go out upon their hunts lest they might be absent on the arrival of the money.

By the plan proposed, the Indian will be relieved from all anxiety and apprehension, for he can purchase of his trader such articles as he may stand in need of and to the full amount of his annuity and at such times as may be most convenient to himself, being thus at perfect liberty to go upon his hunt without even a thought about the annuity or the day of reckoning with [the] trader.

Further, in giving to one person the exclusive privilege of the trade and with authority to credit to the full amount of the annuity, you are not only rendering a most essential service to the Indian by taking away all pretext for his visits to the white settlements (where he would surely fall a prey to the whiskey dealers) but are also in some degree lessening the expences of the Indian Department, as instead of having to encounter the cost and trouble as well as risk of transporting specie to the several agencies, it would only have to pay such drafts as might be drawn upon it by the agents in favor of the different traders. Not a dollar of specie would be required in the Indian country.

NOTE ON BIBLIOGRAPHY

Official Documents

THE MANUSCRIPT inspection reports submitted by Colonel George Croghan to the General-in-chief in Washington are in the War Department records of the National Archives. The reports for 1826, 1827, 1828, 1829, 1831, 1833, 1834, 1835, 1836, and part of 1842 are bound (mixed in with reports of other inspectors) in Inspection Reports, volumes II and III, Office of the Inspector General (Record Group 159). The reports for 1838, 1840, part of 1842, 1843, 1844, and part of 1845 are to be found in Document File: Inspections, Headquarters of the Army (Record Group 108). Part of the 1845 report is filed in Letters Received 1845 (C 311), Adjutant General's Office (Record Group 94).

Other scattered letters and orders referring to Croghan and his inspection duties are found in Letters Received and Letters Sent, Adjutant General's Office (Record Group 94), in Letters Received, Letters Sent, and Document File, Headquarters of the Army (Record Group 108), and in various bound volumes of manuscript General Orders and Special Orders. Two pertinent letters are in the Joel R. Poinsett Papers, in the Historical Society of Pennsylvania. See the footnotes for exact references to material cited.

Essential for an understanding of Croghan's reports are the regulations and orders which determined the duties of the Inspector General and the army activities which he inspected. The Articles of War, which governed the discipline of the army, were estab-

172

lished by an "Act for establishing Rules and Articles for the government of the Armies of the United States," dated April 10, 1806, (*United States Statutes at Large*, II, 359–72) and are reprinted in the various editions of *General Regulations for the Army*. These *General Regulations* were published at Washington, under slightly varying titles, in 1821, 1825, 1835, 1841, and 1847 and at New York in 1857. The edition of 1825 is more detailed than the others, and in many cases the information contained in it seems to be presumed by the later editions. See James B. Fry, *The Different Editions of Army Regulations* (New York, 1876), a small pamphlet which comments briefly on the several editions, and William Winthrop, *Military Law and Precedents* (2d edition, Boston, 1896).

Biographical Material

Material are lacking for a full-scale biography of George Croghan, and information has to be pieced together from many sources. The Croghan Papers in the Draper Collection of the State Historical Society of Wisconsin contain a number of letters dealing with Croghan's War of 1812 experience. These are chiefly letters of Croghan to his father, William Croghan, at Louisville, relating the son's activities during the war. The Croghan Family Papers in the Library of Congress contain considerable correspondence between George Croghan and his brothers William and John, his sister Ann, and her husband, General Thomas Jesup. This correspondence deals with financial matters and other family affairs. The collection also contains some letters concerned with George Croghan's military service. There are a few scattered Croghan items in the Clark Papers (E. G. Voorhis Memorial Collection), Missouri Historical Society. Official letters in the War Department records of the National Archives give information about Croghan's duties as Inspector General and occasionally shed some light on personal affairs.

Most of the published accounts of Croghan deal with his defense of Fort Stephenson in 1813 and with the subsequent hero worship paid him. The "Life of Colonel Croghan," *Portfolio,* 3d series, Vol. V (1815), 212–20, consist of a group of highly complimentary passages written by anonymous contemporaries of Croghan. The brief biography in R. Thomas, *The Glory of America; Comprising Memoirs of the Lives and Glorious Exploits of Some of the Distinguished Officers Engaged in the Late War with Great Britain* (New York, 1836), gives facts about Croghan's early life and service in the War of 1812, but nothing on his later career. Charles Richard Williams, "George Croghan," in *Ohio Archaeological and Historical Publications,* Vol. XII (1903), 375–409, is a flowery address delivered at Fremont, Ohio, on August 1, 1903, on the occasion of the celebration of the ninetieth anniversary of the battle of Fort Stephenson. Lucy Elliot Keeler, "The Croghan Celebration," *ibid.,* Vol. XVI (1907), 1–112, and Lucy Elliot Keeler, "The Centennial of Croghan's Victory," *ibid.,* Vol. XXIII (1914), 1–33, are accounts of the periodic celebrations held on anniversaries of Croghan's defense of Fort Stephenson and contain some biographical data, but almost nothing about Croghan's career as inspector general.

Data about the gold medal awarded to Croghan by Congress in 1835 can be found in *United States Statutes at Large,* IV, 792, and Gales and Seaton's *Debates in Congress,* XI, part 1 (1834–35), columns 236 and 1093. See J. F. Loubat, *The Medallic History of the United States of America, 1776–1876* (New York, 1878), for a description and etching of the medal.

APPENDIX

Colonel Croghan's Tours of Inspection

The following list shows the posts visited by Croghan on his tours of the western forts, according to extant inspection reports. Dates are those indicated on the reports.

1826

Fort Brady	July 9
Fort Mackinac	July 14
Fort Howard	July 27
Camp near Fort Howard	July
Fort Crawford	August
Fort Armstrong	August
Fort Atkinson	October
St. Louis	October

1827

Fort Snelling	May
Fort Armstrong	June 1
New Orleans	June
Fort St. Philip	June
Fort Jackson	
Baton Rouge	
Cantonment Jesup	July
Natchitoches	August

Cantonment Towson	August
Cantonment Gibson	August
Jefferson Barracks	September

1828

Fort Brady	June 21
Fort Mackinac	June
Fort Howard	June
[Also several seaboard posts]	

1829

Cantonment Leavenworth	March 31
Jefferson Barracks	April 13
Cantonment Jesup	May 3
Baton Rouge	May 9
Baton Rouge Arsenal	
Fort St. Philip	May 20
Fort Pike	May 24
Fort Wood	May 25

1831

Fort Brady	June 17
Fort Mackinac	June 21
Fort Howard	June 28
Fort Winnebago	July 3
Fort Snelling	July 15
Fort Crawford	July 20
Fort Armstrong	July 24
Jefferson Barracks	August 6
Cantonment Leavenworth	August 15
Fort Niagara	October 1
Madison Barracks	October 7

1833

Fort Gratiot	September 6
Fort Mackinac	September 19
Fort Howard	September 28
Fort Winnebago	October 10
Fort Crawford	October 15
Jefferson Barracks	November 10

1834

Fort Brady	July 20
Fort Mackinac	July 25
Fort Howard	August 2
Fort Winnebago	August 7
Fort Snelling	August 17
Fort Crawford	August 21
Fort Armstrong	August 25
Jefferson Barracks	August 30
Fort Leavenworth	September 5

1835

Fort Des Moines	December 3

1836

Fort Leavenworth	August 26
Fort Snelling	October 7
Fort Crawford	October 11
Fort Des Moines	October 26

1838

Fort Leavenworth	
Fort Snelling	August 16
Fort Crawford	August 20

Fort Winnebago	August 25
Fort Howard	August 31
Fort Brady	September 12
Fort Mackinac	
Fort Gratiot	September 26
Detroit Arsenal	September 27
Detroit	September 29
Buffalo	October 1

1840

Fort Leavenworth	July
Western Depot	July
St. Louis Arsenal	August
Jefferson Barracks	August
Fort Snelling	September
Fort Crawford	September
Camp Atkinson	September

1842

Detroit	June 16
Detroit Arsenal	June 18
Fort Gratiot	June 21
Fort Brady	June 25
Fort Mackinac	June 28
Fort Winnebago	July 5
Fort Crawford	July 11
Fort Snelling	July 16
Fort Atkinson	July 27
Fort Leavenworth	August 16
St. Louis	
St. Louis Arsenal	
Jefferson Barracks	
Louisville	September 23

1843

Fort Leavenworth	August 12
Jefferson Barracks	August 27
Fort Snelling	September 3
Fort Atkinson	September 7
Fort Crawford	September 11
Fort Winnebago	September 16
Fort Brady	September 29
Fort Mackinac	October 7
Fort Gratiot	October 9
Detroit Barracks	October 11
Buffalo Barracks	October 14
Fort Niagara	October 29
Fort Ontario	October 31
Madison Barracks	November 1
Plattsburg Barracks	November 8
Fort Preble	November 11

1844

Fort Pike	April 12
Fort Wood	April 13
New Orleans Barracks	May 6
Baton Rouge	May 8
Baton Rouge Arsenal	
Fort Jesup	May 14
Camp near Fort Jesup	May 15
Camp Wilkins	May 17
Fort Towson	June 4
Fort Washita	June 19
Fort Smith	June 27
Fort Gibson	July 1
Fort Scott	July 8
Fort Leavenworth	July 12

Jefferson Barracks   July 24
St. Louis Arsenal   July 25

1845

Fort Des Moines   July 25
Fort Snelling   August 6
Fort Atkinson   August 9
Fort Crawford   August 12
Fort Winnebago   August 16
Fort Mackinac   August 23
Fort Brady   August 27
Fort Gratiot   September 2
Detroit Barracks   September 4
Buffalo Barracks   September 10
Fort Niagara   September 13
Fort Ontario   September 15
Madison Barracks   September 16
Plattsburg Barracks   September 20

In 1830 and 1832, Croghan made no inspection tour in the West because of illness in his family. The tour of 1835 was cut short, apparently because of the danger of cholera; in 1837, Croghan was engaged in mustering troops for the Florida war, and he performed a like service in 1846. Data for the years 1839 and 1841 could not be located.

INDEX

Administration of forts: 55–57
Agriculture: *see* farming
Alden, Capt. Bradford R.: 76
Allowances to troops: 55–57
Ames Sword Company: 101n.
Ammunition: *see* ordnance
Annuity payments to Indians: 167, 171
Appearance of men under arms: 147–50
Archer, Inspector General Samuel B.: *xviii*
Arms: *see* small arms, ordnance
Arms racks: 42, 45, 48, 50
Army and Navy Chronicle, on resignations: 156n.
Army regulations: *see General Regulations for the Army*
Arsenals: *xxv; see also* individual arsenals
Articles of War: *xxv,* 172–73; 41st–44th Articles, 124&n.; 66th Article, 108&n.
Artillery posts: 8, 28
Atchison, John, contractor for supplies: 87n.
Atkinson, Gen. Henry: *xxix,* 24

Backus, Capt. Electus: 144
Barbour, James, Secretary of War: *xix*
Barracks: *see* quarters

Baton Rouge Arsenal: *xxx,* 11, 155, 176, 179
Baton Rouge Barracks: *xxix,* 175, 176, 179; abandonment criticized, 11; importance of, 21; state of quarters, 44; mess, 65; hospital, 75; contracts for supplies, 90; discipline, 130; temperance society, 130
Bayonet scabbards: *see* scabbards
Beall, Maj. Benjamin L.: 51, 132
Beaumont, Surgeon William: 70–71
Bedbugs: 43, 46, 48, 51
Beef, in army ration: 68, 82
Belts: 97n., 98, 101
Bibb, Senator George M.: *xvii*
Black Hawk War: 18
Bliss, Maj. John: 152
Books: *see* records *and* medical books
Brady, Gen. Hugh: 7
Branding, as punishment: 120
Bread, in army diet: 64&n.
British Northwest Company: 16, 18
British traders: 37
Brooke, Gen. George M.: 65, 122, 124
Brown, Gen. Jacob: 9n.
Buffalo Barracks: *xxxvi,* 59, 178, 179, 180
Bunks: 42, 44, 45, 46, 48, 50

Canoes, used by Indians: 10

187

ARMY LIFE ON THE WESTERN FRONTIER

was set on the Linotype machine in 11-point Oldstyle Number 7 with two points of space between the lines. The title page is set in Bulmer, a type that goes well with the hard-working and unassuming Oldstyle face. Army Life on the Western Frontier is printed on an antique wove paper.

UNIVERSITY OF OKLAHOMA PRESS : NORMAN